BODY LANGUAGE OF PEOPLE

BEGINNERS GUIDE TO BRAIN SECRETS. HAVE A BODY LANGUAGE MASTERY TO ANALYZE AND INFLUENCE OTHERS. THE BASICS OF PSYCHOLOGY 101.

John Austin

Published by Mybook Self-Publishing Ltd

Table of Contents

Introduction

How would you feel if you were asking a junior colleague at work an important question and he or she merely shrugged his or her shoulders without saying a word?

Naturally, you would conclude the person was being knowingly rude.

Albeit being a rude way to say so, in modern society, a shoulder shrug can be an unspoken way to imply "I don't know". A person could utter the words "I don't know" and shrug his or her shoulders at the same time, which would appear nicer than the response given by a person who merely shrugs his or her shoulders without saying a word. A shrug devoid of words could appear as if the person is implying "I don't know or care".

Because they occupy sensitive societal positions, politicians, public speakers, and successful public figures often go through body language training to learn the proper use of body language when communicating. One instance of wrong body language from someone such as a politician during a public outing could mean a decline in support.

In college, there were incidences where lecturers would get angry with students who were not concentrating or distracting others. The lecturers would then ask such students to get out of class after calling them out. Then the student would be like, "But that's unfair, I didn't even say a word" and the lecturer would reply saying, "You didn't need to say a word, your attitude said it all".

Such a student may not have responded to the lecturer, but the mere fact that their body language was sending out signals the lecturer found disrespectful after the lecturer had called them out meant the student had to leave class.

Control and use of non-verbal communication including body language is a critical must-have skill for all of us because it holds the key to building or destroying relationships.

Another example that shows the importance of body language is that of two waiters, A and B who serve you at restaurants without saying a word to you and while you hand Waiter A a nice tip, you refuse to tip waiter B because you do not like his or her 'attitude'. Unconsciously, it is not that waiter's attitude you dislike, it is his or her body language.

You may be a very hard worker only to discover no one in the office likes you. You then may start wondering why. The answer to this riddle could perhaps be you have a snobbish attitude that displays in how you non-verbally interact and communicate with others.

One thing I remember clearly is that people used to say I look like a very mean and unapproachable person. This often made me wonder why because I am friendly and easy to talk to. However, because that is what my body language said, others did not bother looking behind the mask. Because my body language was negative, they assumed I was a mean person who would probably insult them if they dared say hi.

You do not have bad luck; neither is your lack of designer apparel that makes it hard for others to approach and interact with you. The problem is your body language-you are unintentionally sending out the wrong signals. Although unintentional, your negative body language is off putting to those around you. Not to worry though, in later sections, you shall learn proper body language ethics that will help you attract people and build strong relationships.

Before we get to that, it is only fair we start by cultivating an in-depth understanding of the puzzle that is body language.

Chapter 1 Psychology 101

Psychologically, body language is the art of communicating without using words. It can be anything you do or any action you take that someone else takes to mean something. Body language is not always intentional; most times, majority of us often fail to realize that others are reading meanings to what we do even when we do not utter a single word.

Each human thinks of him or herself as an amateur psychologist. We all think we can figure people out or read people just by watching them. This is why people conduct interviews; they believe that just by watching you for a few minutes, they can learn a thing or two about you- your personality and possibly, your character.

Human beings are also smart. When you know others are watching and observing you, you continuously work to present yourself in a certain way. You try to control and manage the impressions others have of you.

Managing impressions is the essence of body language- using the right body language to manage the message you send and the impression you leave on others.

Importance Of Body Language

Reasons why you should learn effective body language are as many as the lines on your palm. Below are a number of reasons why learning body language is such an important undertaking:

Detecting Insincerity: By properly studying the art of body language communication, you can easily detect when someone is lying or 'cooking' the truth. For instance, when someone avoids eye contact or stammers a lot while communicating, it might mean the person is being insincere. Body language is honest and that is why law enforcement arms of government use it often. Your words may hide the truth, but it is very difficult to hide your body language.

Reinforcement of Words: You can use body language to render more impact to, and reinforce your words. That way, you get people to pay attention to you when you are communicating with them.

Knowing When to Stop: Body language can also help you detect when a person is uncomfortable with a particular conversation or when someone does not like what you are saying. When you know this, you can easily change the topic of conversation.

Expression of Feelings: Another very important use of body language communication is that you can use it to express feelings during communication. A person may say yes when what he or she really means is no. By understanding body language, you detect real intentions without the need for words.

Confidence: You can use body language to show confidence. This is especially important for leaders because followers have to view their leaders as confident and in control. Body language signals such as breaking a sweat, stammering, or being jittery while addressing followers may send out signals that a leader is very unconfident, which may affect the level of trust followers have in such leaders.

Games: If you play games like poker, body language can be a very useful skill to learn because it can give you an idea of your opponent's state of mind and his or her next move.

Chapter 2 Learning to interpret body language

Learning to interpret body language is a very suitable ability when it comes to dealing with people. Movements are part of human communication. Subconscious movements represent 93% of human communication. The speech is only 7%. You can guess someone thinking process or mood if he knows how to interpret body language. These actions are usually unconscious. They can be a response to a situation or a biological reaction. Facial gestures, hand movements, and posture are ordered in kinetics, the learning of human movements in a statement.

These physical expressions are used to support or refer to a statement of awareness. Talking to people, there are signs to watch out for. These characters may indicate a negative setting. These negative reactions can be perceived as unpleasant if the person being analyzed is not true or has no interest. Attention should be paid to body language gestures, such as eye position, posture and hand movements. Much of eye contact and the absence of this can mean ailments. Too much attention can indicate a lack of trust. This lack of trust allows the person to pay full attention. Leaning also means distrust. This action means that the person wants to get away. Scratching the jaw or touching the earlobes is a sign of disbelief.

Body language is also used to indicate a level of comfort and intimacy. A distance of eight feet or more indicates a public distance. This type of disposal is used in public functions, e.g., to watch a movie or listen to a conference. It can be used in large groups of observers. Four to eight feet denote a social distance. Newly introduced people maintain this distance. Close enough to make contacts, but not too close to mark associations. Friends are a meter and a half away. This means a level of trust. The shortest distances that these are reserved for people close to the individual. Family, close friends and lovers are allowed on this route. This area of proximity means intimacy and a higher level of trust.

These are some of the signs you should keep in mind when talking with another person. It's easy to lie or be honest, so never trust words alone. You can use your understanding of body language to your advantage and succeed in your career, in your relationships, and in all kinds of activities in which you interact with people.

Body language is what we call a nonverbal or tacit way of communicating and interacting with another person. Being gestures, gestures, and other physical signs, body language is like a mirror that informs us about the thoughts and feelings of the other person in response to our words and actions.

In case you think that learning to read and use body language is not so important, let me show the actual statistics of the messages we receive from someone when we meet.

☐   8% of the information we receive comes from what they really say.

☐   37% of the information we receive comes from the tone of voice, inflection, and speed of your voice.

☐   The incredible 55% of the information we receive comes from your body language.

Imagine that you could leave a great impression of work, business, and love by having the knowledge and ability to read other people's thoughts. It is a very powerful tool for a successful life and general personality development.

Remember that it is equally important to send the correct signals and eliminate the incorrect signals from your own body, as this is very useful for reading other people's body language.

Keep in mind that many signals have different meanings depending on the individual and the scenario. Always look for 3 or 4 signals that contain the same message or the inconsistent signal at once. Remember, when evaluating these signals. Below are some of the common body language cues.

Body language signals:

Darting Eyes:

☐   Scam

☐   Lying down

- ☐   Trap

- ☐   Doesn't look you in the eye

- ☐   Dishonest

- ☐   Cheat

- ☐   Lack of trust

Displaced eyes:

- ☐   Scam

- ☐   Lack of trust

- ☐   Look into the eyes without looking:

- ☐   Self-confident

- ☐   Insurance

Rigid:

- ☐   Signs of aggression

- ☐   In spite of

Extended students:

- ☐   Show great interest

- ☐   Centered

- ☐   About drugs

To bite nails:

- [ ] Feeling insecure

- [ ] Nervous

Run your fingers through your hair:

- [ ] Cleaning

- [ ] Frustration

Drumming fingers:

- [ ] Thought

- [ ] Impatient

Stand up:

- [ ] Insurance

- [ ] Show respect

Contracted posture:

- [ ] Low self-esteem

- [ ] Low confidence

- [ ] Boring

Red cheeks:

- [ ] Feel ashamed

- [ ] Show interest in another person

Strong tremor of the legs:

☐ Nervousness

☐ Conception

☐ Enthusiasm

Cut hands:

☐ Aggression

☐ Antagonize another person

☐ Point the finger at another person:

☐ Domain

☐ Aggression

☐ Authoritarianism

High flicker rate:

☐ Nervousness

☐ Qualification

☐ Pluck:

☐ Possible hoax

☐ Indecision

The eyes look and wander:

☐ Bored by the current situation or conversation

- ☐ Think about other things

- ☐ Go to

  Closed fist:

- ☐ Aggression

- ☐ Very tense

- ☐ Challenging or triumphant

  Crossed arms:

- ☐ Defensiveness

- ☐ Closed mind

- ☐ Possible rejection

  Open arms:

- ☐ Accessible

- ☐ Feels potentially vulnerable

- ☐ Open hands:

- ☐ Open heart

- ☐ Defenses below

The ability to read the signals of others is a sure way to communicate effectively. By observing how people move and gesture, you can directly address their emotions. You can see the intensity of a person's feelings through their attitude. You can see the type of mood of the other person by the speed of their gestures. When you have an idea of a person's emotions, you can respond appropriately to situations, since you are prevented and prepared for what happens next.

Take fifteen to twenty minutes a day to study and observe other people's gestures and realize their own gestures. A great learning environment is everywhere where many people meet and interact. One of the best places to observe human gestures will be an airport where people openly express enthusiasm, anger, grief, happiness, impatience, and many other emotions through gestures. Other great places include social events, business meetings, and parties.

Another excellent way to learn nonverbal communication is to watch television. Turn down the volume and try to understand what is happening by looking at the image alone without looking at the subtitles. If you increase the volume every five minutes, you can check how accurate your nonverbal readings are, and soon you can watch a complete program without sound or subtitles, and see exactly what happens to the deaf.

Common Language Of The Body To Avoid

Many people use body language to send messages to their neighbors. Body language can affirm to others whenever we are happy, sad, angry, disgusted, silly, flirtatious and more.

However, body language can sometimes send an incorrect message. When you meet new people, it is important to present the correct messages with your body language. This means that you know your body language with a certain degree of accuracy. Consider some common speech disorders.

Reading body language poorly is a well-known mistake, and most of us are victim of at one time or the other. Let's have a look at this illustration, the young man leaning against the wall of the supermarket, with his leg bent back and his foot propped against the wall. He wears a large, thick coat and seems out of place as if he did not belong there. As it happens, he interprets his body language as a moron, unemployed and wasting his time. But you don't think he's waiting to be taken to work. You just misunderstood this young man's body language and misunderstood his behavior. Now let's look at your body language and how people could misunderstand you.

As we have all heard, the eyes are the windows of the soul, and eye contact can send an incorrect message about you if it is not used while listening or speaking. Most people perceive the lack of eye contact as a form of disinterest. Even if you are interested in the other person, that person who is speaking can misunderstand you and end the meeting and conversation. Another common mistake in body language is to cross your arms or place something in front of you, such as a book, a chair or another object. For some people, crossing their arms or placing something in front of you sends the message that you are inaccessible because you have placed a barrier in front of you.

Some men cross their arms when they talk to another without really knowing that this is the case. We have all seen a self-confident man do this when he hears us or speaks with another person or us. Their conversation and attitude are pleasant, but those arms crossed. What do you say; Silly and immature is another form of body language, but it has its time and place. Having fun and hanging out with good and well-established friends in the park can be an acceptable time and an acceptable place to hang out. But if you are in a social function and are trying to meet new people, certainly, this is not the time for this type of nonverbal communication. If you meet new people, it may be beneficial to show your humorous side, but if you become silly, you probably won't attract new people. In fact, you may receive looks of disgust from those around you.

An incorrect attitude is a common mistake. Crouch down and for women crossed legs can like

Not smiling at new contacts is a sure way to dissuade people. It is a guaranteed way to make people avoid it, even if it doesn't really matter to you. If you don't smile, people will perceive you as inaccessible. So smile and win some friends! Now you know the most common mistakes in body language to avoid. You have a lot to laugh at!

Have you ever feel in a way whereby you were almost sure that the person you spoke with lied to you? You wanted to believe the words that came out of his mouth, but your gut said something was wrong. His eye movement, facial expressions, and body movement simply did not reflect his verbal communication. Her body language, known as nonverbal communication, had betrayed her, although they thought she had been deceived.

The capability to understand a person's body language can be a great advantage to you. Can you imagine communicating with someone and understanding what kind of message you are trying to convey before opening your mouth to say a single word? If you go one step further, what would happen if you could use your own body language to convey your message even before beginning verbal communication? If at first glance you are sending messages in body language such as "I am sure," "I am interested," "I am bored", "I am not interested," you can save a lot of time and problems.

Many communications experts believe that 50-70% of all communication is nonverbal. Just when we stop, sit down, talk and walk, everyone says something about us and reflects what really happens inside. Remember that there is not a single expression in body language that gives you a complete understanding of a person's message or situation. Everyone has their own body language. Do not jump to conclusions immediately. You are not clairvoyant!

With this in mind, you can create some common detectors for later analysis so you can infer what communication in body language someone shows you. For example, if someone lies to you, he could:

- Try to avoid eye contact by looking the other way and avoiding complete eye contact or making rapid eye movements to and from you.

- Rinse your throat frequently or change your tone of voice.

- Increase respiratory rate.

- The color of your face or neck turns red.

- Annoying, like the constant change in the movement of the foot, which shows that they are uncomfortable.

- Excessive flash.

- Offer a fake smile, no expression in your eyes.

- Avoid answering a direct question (politicians have perfected this question).

These are all signs that someone is lying to you, but as mentioned earlier, don't jump too fast to any conclusions. It could be your character to avoid eye contact or restlessness. They can be shy and insecure and feel uncomfortable while they are together.

Attraction Of Body Reading Language

When it comes to taking love interests, sometimes the other sex just doesn't understand. Don't be frustrated; just try some simple and effective body language tricks. Everyone uses body language all the time. We can say that we are happy, confused, disturbed or interested! But knowing what your body says is especially important when it comes to love interests. These body language indicators put your unexpressed communication skills into shape.

Occasionally lick your lips to draw attention to these beautiful wrinkles. You should use this very rarely, but occasionally lick your lips to draw attention to one of the sexiest parts of your body and show that you are interested.

Synchronize with your love interest. Being physically synchronized with someone indicates that you are also synchronized with him spiritually. Imitate some of their movements, for example. For example, drink your drink or bow down when they do. Don't overdo that. You are not supposed to be a literal mirror; you are just trying to suggest to your subconscious that both are in tune. Moving towards someone is another sign that you care about him. When you touch or rely on a love interest in your arm, your desire to be closer mentally and physically becomes evident.

Make latent eye contact. When you look at this strange seducer, you know that you are dressed. But this should not be a second class competition. Just give them the look that is long enough so they can look at them. The sexy look also works closely. If you two are already talking, make sure they know they have your full attention. You don't have to look at them, you don't have to look around each time or check the door when it opens. It's a way to show them that you care and what they say.

The flirting tips quickly capture a man's attention. If you occasionally remove your hair from your face or throw it away, you can attract great flirtatious attention in an excellent way. Another great trick is to slightly bow your head when you hit it. If you give them that look, you'll be fascinated and interested.

Place your body in your direction. Center your shoulders on the person you are interested in. When you sit and cross your legs, showing the knee sends them the same signal. It says "I am interested in you and you have my attention."

Touch or caress an object in front of you. Be sure to keep this underestimated. Slightly stroking your wine glass or touching your leg while sitting is a sign that you want to touch the person in front of you.

Would you like to show that you are interested in someone? Let your body say everything. Body language can make things happen to someone you just met or turn a friend into a love interest. If you use body language, you can say that you are interested without having to say anything.

We are often attracted to people with a good personality. A good personality shows the confidence in you that attract other people. In public, our body language plays an important role in the impression of the audience. The biggest challenge in public speaking is maintaining an effective attitude that results from good emotional intelligence. The way we deliver our speech consists of two components: visual and verbal. I think the visual component is usually more important for viewers. This mainly includes body language, posture, eye contact and facial expression of a person. More than half of his impact as a speaker depends on his body language. Can you control the words you say, have control over what you say with your body language?

Body language includes gestures, postures and facial expressions. When you speak with a large audience, all eyes are on you, so it is important to have good body language at all times. In public, your positive body language helps you build a reputation for the audience. It also helps your listeners to focus on you and what you say.

Verbal expression means using the right words

Look energetic and confident while sitting. Sitting straight in your chair, with your back straight, your feet flat on the floor and your hands open on the table makes you feel comfortable.

Avoid an exaggerated expression that can confuse the public.

Get up and introduce yourself to the audience. It is important to keep your hands at your sides or keep them carefully on the podium. Facilitate these projects.

Do not hesitate on the podium as this can distract even the most interested audience.

Avoid being behind the music stand, as it separates you from the audience while you want to bring it closer.

The height should be adjusted according to your needs.

Look at each part of the room. From right to left, from front to back, to interest each person in the audience.

Use your hands to underline a point and lessen pressure.

Do not keep your hands on your back or in your pockets. This shows nervousness.

If you cross your arms, you are not interested in communication.

No matter how much you speak in public, but if you prowl, you will surely leave the worst impression on the audience.

Keep your head up with your chin up. The chin augmentation allows you have the feeling of being in control.

Measure your gestures according to the size of the room.

Their movements must be wide and fluid, not rushed or abrupt.

The feet should point forward. If you don't gesture, your hands should sit silently at your sides.

You can move, but remember to intervene with silence from time to time.

Try to freeze your face from the beginning. Smile during the audience greeting and at other times during the speech.

Sometimes, short-lived spokesmen decide to move forward and be closer to the audience rather than clinging to the music stand to appear tall.

In fact, it is difficult for most people to be alone in front of a group of people. It is something strange that creates anxiety, tension and butterflies in the stomach. Being natural is not the abbreviation of it. We have to make an extra effort and use all our speech and presentation skills to be more expressive and influential. It is worth recharging the batteries, as this depends largely on our body language. Work on your body language to make you have the opportunity to speak in public and stand out. If you have adequate body language, proper movements, eye contact, gestures, and posture, you are on your way to public speaking successfully.

Chapter 3 Evaluation criteria

Surely you have already experienced the phenomenon that a word that you've learned just now to understand, suddenly permanently "turns up." It's as if newspapers, radio, television, books, and fellow human beings have conspired to use this vocabulary all the time. In fact, in all likelihood, the word had previously been used just as often, but we have overheard or missed it.

Something similar will happen to you now with regard to the body language signals. You will be amazed at the abundance of information that comes to you from all sides! Maybe you have already noticed this effect. But you do not just want to perceive more, but also use these perceptions practically.

However, if you want to evaluate, analyze, interpret, or even refine (please do not judge), you need criteria. Without standards one cannot measure, without a prescription of what one wants to examine, no results can arise. Our generic terms posture, facial expressions, gestures, distance, and tone were perceptual criteria that serve us (similar to auxiliary lines) to make us an "image." If we can now perceive and verbalize a signal, then we have taken the necessary first step with it: we have described (see preface). However, our verbalization does not say anything about the signal's rating.

But what do we want to know? Which priorities do we want to set? What can we pay attention to?

Any "statement" that someone will give you now will change the way you and others see you in the future, and so on. You can strongly influence this. Therefore, I would like to ask you to regard the following train of thought as just one possible approach. There are others. Determine your own reactions when reading. Be especially critical. Because in this chapter, in fact, it's about a philosophical question: "What should one pay attention to when judging oneself and others?" One person considers spontaneity to be an important criterion, another honesty, and the other places great value on self-discipline (so that he will rate spontaneity differently from the one that seemed so valuable to them). Further, someone may find it important that the observed signals correspond to his notions of "good behavior" because he considers politeness an important criterion. Such a person is more likely to judge the other's yawning as "negative," especially when executed without a hand or even to interpret this signal as rudeness towards him, that is, as a "hostile" signal.

Ultimately everyone has to decide for themselves which priorities to set, but often a discussion about possible criteria helps to define their own more precisely!

Honesty / Sincerity

This is a criterion that is consistently considered by most seminars participants to be the "main criterion." I would like to advise caution here. First, how honest is "honest"? Second, do you have a clear answer to the question of whether "absolute" honesty could sometimes be very hurtful, and to what extent it should be sought after? Third, are you so sure you never lie to yourself or others?!?! (Be it insecurity or embarrassment, be it in the form of a "polite" lie, or because you may not want to believe something?) Interestingly enough, I have often found that those who put so much emphasis on catching others in the event of lies, not always understanding it with the truth. Here is the psychoanalytic conclusion that they, because they deduce themselves from others, are so afraid of the dishonesty of others. Also, if someone lies out of fear of the consequences, or because he does not want to hurt another, then the motives are completely different. The "truth fanatics" usually ignore this, precisely because they have not given enough thought to the criterion of honesty!

Congruence / Incongruence

Of course, every signal always refers to the situation in which the looking person is currently located. Incongruence can therefore mean:

1. A discrepancy to the spoken words.

2. A discrepancy between an observed signal and our expectation: Assuming you give someone a present and expect a pleasing response, but see that the other

is disappointed or depressed. This would be such an incongruence.

3. A discrepancy between an observed signal and our expectation can also lead to pseudo-incongruence if the other one has no idea what we might have expected. In the example above, the recipient knows that the giver hopes he will be happy. It is different when you expect a reaction that the others cannot guess. Either because you think he has some information that he (still) does not have. Or because it comes from a different culture and will, therefore, send "unexpected" signals that may seem incongruent to us, even though they are not (in his view).

4. A discrepancy to the person. Franz Josef Strauss was expected in certain situations, so to speak, certain signal groups. The better you know a person, the more likely you are to be able to predict your analog signals. However, if these are completely different now, then we say that the person is not "herself" today. This is what we mean by incongruence with the person.

5. Lately, there is an incongruence factor in gestures that, strictly speaking, are not. Some people wave completely unmotivated in the air or hit the table in a steady rhythm, although they do not say anything that

should be "underpinned." These analog signals seem to have no relation to the words and are therefore also perceived as incongruent.

Spontaneity / Self-Discipline

The more spontaneous a reaction, the less thoughtful it is. If honesty and sincerity are important, spontaneity will be more "positive" than self-discipline. Now the signals are always "embedded" in the overall situation, so that there may well be moments when free, open, informal, spontaneous behavior may seem "more positive" than restrained, disciplined behavior. Furthermore, those who always consider spontaneity to be "better" in case of doubt should be aware that tactlessness was also very spontaneous. Tactlessness is just a reaction that someone sent out before thinking about his words! That's why I sometimes silently amuse myself about a person I know who on the one hand demands that one should always be spontaneous, but at the same time very lightly offended if her brother violates her spontaneously with one of his "indiscretions." From this, we can once again see how difficult it is to create "absolute" standards for assessing body language signals (or standards for assessing each behavior!).

Positive / Negative

Of course, we perceive individual signals as "good" or "bad," i.e. we classify them immediately and usually unconsciously as "positive" or "negative." It must be clear that this is an extremely subjective description of the world and our fellow human beings. Whether a behavior is spontaneous or controlled, can be measured with a different scale than "good" or "bad" signals. So, if someone classifies a yawn of the other as disinterest and thus as negative, then he has judged very subjective. First, he assumes that the other yawns only when he has no interest (maybe he closes it to others?)! Secondly, he may feel the signal "negative" because it is "rude." Especially with the label "rude," one must be aware that all the rules of behavior are fixed on certain cultures and certain epochs of time. In Erasmus von ROTTERDAM, for example: "When two fingers fall down on the ground with two fingers, it must immediately be kicked out with the foot," both our two-fingered sniveling was considered rude (negative) also the leakage of nasal mucus. A second example with ROTTERDAM, however, has survived the times so far and could still be in a book of manners today: "Some.... have to scratch their heads or drill around in their teeth or gesticulate wildly with their hands and play with the knife (at a table). Or they have to cough and snort and spit. All this basically comes from a peasant embarrassment and looks like some kind of weirdness." One final example is intended to clarify two things: First, how little conscious is one's behavior or signals that seem "wrong" to be immediately negatively classified, i.e. emotionally angry or injured responding to them. This reaction is best shown by those norms that you normally do not talk about anymore. They are so natural (programmed) that we are already upset when someone brings them up. Secondly, the more often someone has to deal with people from other (sub-) cultures, the greater the danger that he will be quick as lightning unconsciously finds certain signals "bad" and lets them perceive them negatively-as long as he is not aware of this danger and can stand up to it. The last example:

"Some prescribe that the boy 'retains a tight buttocks blasts,' but one can thereby contract an illness."

How seldom do we consciously think that one has to hold back himself these days? This is clearly a norm that is hardly ever verbalized. Nevertheless, we react immediately if someone does not obey them, or if someone, after "it" happened to him, does not immediately send the "corresponding" analog signals, that is to say: dismayed at how embarrassing he is! But once you have the opportunity to sit with Bedouin, you would be angry with these people if you looked upset because these people do not accept your standard ... so it would be best to have this permanent classification in "good" or "positive" (or "negative") and therefore, we could get it under control. For one thing, because we always feel annoyed or hurt when we have a negative signal. This means that we are now producing combat hormones and wasting unnecessary energies into the process of having a "rage in the stomach." To a lesser extent, this also applies to any slight annoyance of course. On the other hand, because some signals in the eyes of the other cannot be "negative" at all if they start from different norms and customs than we do. However, these feelings of displeasure on our part are accompanied by negative signals, which we now send on a relationship level, which of course worsens the relationship and "poisons" the atmosphere of conversation. The "poison" are our fighting hormones.

Joke And Irony

Just this is an example where the words of the driving instructor should not be taken "seriously" when he says: "Always let the clutch pedal soar abruptly, which is enormously good for the transmission."

Now there are people who take everything very seriously. That's why the idea does not come to them, someone might want to make a joke. If the "ironic tone" is hinted at only slightly, it may well be that such persons "fall for" the digital signals. That's why the environment loves to "hug" them. For someone like that, the question of how serious someone might have meant something is a useful criterion. In particular, when one has more to do with people whose "dry humor" is accompanied by such weak analog signals that only a trained person will hear the irony or sarcasm. But sarcasm can be so hurtful when it uttered evil things in a tone that sounds so "sober," so "rational," so "objective."

You could list more criteria. But, first of all, there are many more in subgroups already mentioned and, secondly, unfortunately, we cannot go into the ethical systems that must be subject to any criteria choice. Our little discussion should only help you to determine the criteria by which you can judge. Of course, this decision is up to you! Another criterion will be discussed before we turn to the signals themselves:

Only A Single Signal?

There are situations in which success control is impossible. For example, if we judge the analog signals of a politician on television, or if we do not want to interrupt someone. An essential criterion is the question that on how many (or which) signals you support your assessment? Although there are sometimes individual signals that already have meaningfulness (we still come back to them), in general, they represent an exceptional case. Because the basic rule is rather:

A signal alone has no significance!

In particular, this applies to "small" signals such as the lifting of an eyebrow, which can have a variety of causes. Therefore, I consider statements by some authors to be dangerous, who already want to interpret the hand-in-the-bag plug-in alone, or who claim that just the way someone holds his cigarette already has clear explanatory power. Maybe such a signal can give us a hint, but just a hint, not the sole one! For example, brandishing a cigarette with a burning cigarette in front of your eyes may be an indication that he may not respect someone else's genital area. If we now include this hint in our targeted observation, it may be that we notice other signals pointing in the same direction. Or else he often intervenes in the "space of another" (both literally and figuratively), or else he takes objects of others without asking, i.e. only such a signal group can contain a certain significance.

Exceptions to this rule are pronounced, strongly striking gestures that are clearly in contradiction to what has been said. Furthermore, all abrupt changes in body posture are considered an exception to the rule. As a conclusion to the interpretation, before we tackle these, one more word of the great geneticist Birdwhistell.

No physical posture or movement has an exact meaning per se. Body language and languages are interdependent.

Ultimately, this means nothing else than that we must simultaneously perceive and describe the signals of the content and relationship levels if we want to "interpret" a gesture or another non-speech signal.

Chapter 4 Two Hemispheres of our Brain

I'd like to begin the discussion on the two hemispheres of the brain with a little parable that I wrote, I will let it speak for itself before continuing:

The Two Sages

A young Seeker of the truth traveled many miles to the foot of a mountain where two sages lived that held the mysteries of the universe.

As he approached the foot of the mountain he saw a simple structure made of wood. It was basically a wooden floor with four beams holding a wooden roof above it. Standing in front of the two sages who both sat cross-legged, one in complete silence and the other chanting softly to himself, was a small boy.

As the Seeker approached the small boy spoke: "Who is it that approaches the Sages of Enlightenment?"

The Seeker stopped in his tracks and responded: "I am Joe Lostsoul, I am here to speak to the great sages and learn the truth of reality."

The boy cocked his head then replied: "I didn't ask your name Seeker, I asked who you are."

To this, the Seeker was at a loss.

After some thought, he then proposed, "I am a man from San Jose, California and a citizen of the United States of America."

"I didn't ask your sex or where you lived Seeker, I asked who you are." responded the boy boredly.

"I am a software engineer and I wish to consult the sages."

"I didn't ask your profession Seeker, I asked who you are."

The Seeker paused and considered his response and the boy sat patiently waiting. Finally, after much consideration, the Seeker replied: "I am the son of my parents Lilly and Jacob Lostsoul."

"I didn't ask your lineage Seeker, I asked who you are." the boy's demeanor didn't alter in the slightest nor was his tone angry or jeering. It was factual and calm. The Seeker was again at a loss.

The boy sat patiently with a very compelling smile on his face. He seemed quite disinterested in whether or not the Seeker was going to speak further. The Seeker was running out of things to suggest and stood silent for a moment before the boy. After a long while in silence, the boy finally spoke: "You're getting closer Seeker..."

The Seeker had no idea what the boy was referring to and this only added to his confusion. What answer did the boy need to hear? The Seeker could think of no other way to describe who he was to the boy.

He felt a deep need to speak to the sages but could not solve this riddle that barred his entrance. The boy sat patiently waiting but the Seeker was out of ideas.

"I'm afraid I do not know the answer to that question" the Seeker finally said in resignation.

"Then you may enter" replied the boy and who then stepped aside.

The Seeker was confused but didn't want to wait around for the boy to change his mind and so moved quickly past the boy and approached the sages.

The sage on the left was rocking slightly back and forth and mumbling to himself while the sage on the right sat completely still and silent. The Seeker was consumed with excitement in anticipation of finally receiving the truth. He fell to his knees before the sages and prostrated himself before them.

"Oh great Sages of Enlightenment, I have come seeking the truth! What is the truth of the universe and who am I in it?"

The sage on the left answered immediately "You are the greatest soul ever to reside in a body."

The sage on the right remained silent.

The Seeker responded, "Oh wise Left Sage, I don't understand does that mean that all other souls are less than I am?"

"Nothing in this universe is greater than you are. You are the center from which all the universe spins. You are the hub of the wheel. Nothing of any importance happens that does not relate to you" continued the Left Sage. The Right Sage again remained silent.

"But how can this be, I will die one day and I will no longer exist!"

"When you die the universe dies with you. Without you there is nothing." replied the Left Sage.

"I don't understand, did the universe exist before me?"

"No, before you, there was nothing. No one." the Left Sage continued.

"How can that be? What about my parents?"

"Your parents exist to create you, without you they have no existence." replied the Left Sage.

"That doesn't make any sense to me. How can that be?"

"You are the center of the universe, nothing exists without you."

The Seeker was baffled by the Left Sage and looked over to the Right Sage who sat quietly and motionlessly. In his eyes was a depth and calmness and a hint of compassion and the Seeker was quite calmed by the gaze of the Right Sage.

The Left Sage went back to mumbling to himself while the Seeker took in all he had heard. After a moment the Seeker finally turned to the Left Sage:

"So, when I die the entire universe dies with me?"

"Yes, it is yours. Take what you will from it. All belongs to you" replied the Left Sage who immediately went back to mumbling to himself under his breath.

"So I can take anything I want at any time?"

"Anything that you desire, take it, it is yours."

"But how can I do that?"

"You reach out and grasp it. Do what is needed. Take what is yours."

"Anything!?"

"Anything." the Left Sage went back to mumbling to himself.

"But what happens when it is consumed or if it no longer satisfies me?"

"Then find something else to satisfy you and take it instead."

"But what if other people try to stop me from taking it?"

"Then they are wrong and they should be punished. Devise a way to punish them and implement it."

"That doesn't seem fair."

"Anything you do in that cause will be right and just."

This seemed odd and the Seeker turned to the Right Sage whose gaze was constant and compelling but who remained silent.

"But what if they fight back?"

"Then bring greater force than they are able to and overcome their resistance."

"What if I am unable to do so?"

"Then you will be a failure and you will diminish. And if you go, so does the entire universe. You don't want that do you?"

"No, no I don't."

"Then do as I say Seeker" concluded the Left Sage with great forcefulness and confidence.

The Seeker stood and absorbed what was said. The Left Sage went back to his mumbling. The Seeker felt emboldened and ready to seek confrontation in a world of potential competitors who might wish to take what was rightfully his. He turned and began to leave when an idea hit him and his feeling of greatness dwindled immediately.

He turned back to the Left Sage "Wait, how can this be true!? There had to be a universe before me and there must be one after I am gone!"

"No, there was nothing before you and nothing will remain after you are gone."

"That makes no logical sense."

"It is true and that is all you need know" replied the Left Sage who went back to his mumbling.

The Seeker remained unsatisfied and turned to the Right Sage who gazed up at him with a depth in his eyes and a kindness in his smile.

"Do you have nothing to say on this subject?"

The Right Sage was silent and remained motionless but quite alert.

"You have nothing you can offer me in my pursuit of truth?"

"That one says nothing, ignore him, he knows nothing of the truth" mumbled the Left Sage who then continued, "Go and do as I say."

The Seeker remained unconvinced and gazed at the Right Sage.

"I know you know something, what can you show me?"

"All he knows is what he sees, hears, feels, smells, tastes, and touches in this present moment. He has no wisdom of what is important. Go and listen only to me and return with all that your heart desires" demanded the Left Sage.

The Seeker hesitated. Something inside him knew that the Right Sage had something for him. The Right Sage made no motion toward him nor movement of any kind but held his gaze with a look of love and compassion. The look alone was enough to make the Seeker calm and without need for a brief moment.

"Don't fall for that parlor trick, it's just a fleeting feeling. Go and take what is yours!" demanded the Left Sage slowly becoming angry. "Do you not have the common sense to take what is yours!?" he continued and his anger was rising to fury as he continued, "WHAT KIND OF FOOL ARE YOU!? DO YOU WISH TO BE A NOBODY!? A NOTHING!?"

Just then the Right Sage offered his hand.

"Don't take that it's one of his parlor tricks. Hocus pocus, it's not real..." warned the Left Sage.

The Seeker looked into the eyes of the Right Sage and saw a peaceful and calm gaze staring back at him. Trust filled him implicitly and he found he had no reason not to reach out and take the hand offered by the Right Sage.

The instant their hands made contact boundaries of his body vanished and he could no longer define the limits of his skin and body as opposed to the energy that surrounded him. His consciousness expanded to fill the space which had no apparent bounds. He knew, without thoughts and without words, by direct experience that he was one with all things and that individual things were, in fact, an illusion and that there was no difference between the energy that made up his body and the energy that made up everything around him.

He felt peace and harmony vibrate throughout his body which had expanded to become the entire space around him. He looked down and his human body looked small and insignificant and he felt that there was no way he could squeeze himself back into that little vessel.

Moreover, he knew he didn't want to. Why would anyone choose to feel small and insignificant when the truth was just the opposite? He had found universal truth and it came from listening to the lies of the Left Sage and experiencing firsthand the truth of the Right Sage.

The comparison between the two states allowed him to perceive reality in a way he never thought possible. He had reached Enlightenment.

In this parable, the Left Sage and the Right Sage are in fact representations of the consciousness of the Left and Right Hemispheres of the brain.

In the search for the answers to the question of the mystery of the "self" the two hemispheres are quite different in their approaches. The Left Hemisphere is always ready to offer hypotheses and theories about who you are, and always with itself as the center of importance. The Right Hemisphere, however, existing outside of the realm of language and time, is silent but constant and when listened to will offer you the experience of the entire universe as yourself.

The Middle Way that the Buddha talked about many years ago comes from feeling both perceptions simultaneously. Enlightenment is the process of sensing through the Right Hemisphere as the primary perception focal point, whereas we seem to be naturally inclined to do so through the Left. Because of how the Left Hemisphere perceives the universe, it makes one feel small and constantly "at war" with the environment. Peace and ease come from the serenity of the Right Hemisphere which knows by direct experience that it is one with all things and that the universe and itself are inseparable.

Why We Need Two Perceptions

One of the primary reasons why we need two perceptions is because we fall into two evolutionary roles as predator and as prey.

When we are predators, we need to objectify the universe. We need to bias our own form over others and seek out other forms to "prey upon" or steal energy from to gather it to our own form. If we saw everything as "us" we would be very hampered in this biological need and so we need to "switch" to a perception of the world where there are adversarial "others" that may or may not serve as a food source for our further survival.

Our Left Hemisphere provides us in this endeavor with a sense of separation from the world. It gives us an ability to see images as individual objects so that we can "pick out" details of high interest. We can then to choose whether or not to pursue them as food.

However, once satiated we switch to a "safety in numbers" approach to survival used by prey animals. Many pairs of eyes increase our survival rate by spotting potential predators and then alarming the rest of the group of their approaches.

In such an environment a perception of a group "us" is needed that includes a very empathic structure for bonding. And so it is clear that there must be a part of our perception that sees the company of others as a pleasant situational experience. Otherwise we simply would not seek out such environments.

Our Right Hemisphere helps us out in this. It allows us the ability to meld with a group consciousness, or rather to let go of a single sense of "me" in place of a much wider sense of "us." This comes from the Right Hemisphere's perception that no longer feels like an isolated form in a sea of other forms.

Chapter 5 INFJ

INFJ (thoughtful, instinctive, feeling, and judging) is one of the 16 character types recognized by the Myers-Briggs Type Indicator (MBTI). Now and again alluded to as the "Promoter" or the "Romantic," individuals with INFJ characters are inventive, delicate, and minding. INFJs are normally saved however exceptionally delicate to how others feel. They are ordinarily hopeful, with high good models and a solid spotlight on what's to come. INFJs appreciate considering profound subjects and pondering the significance of life. The INFJ type is said to be one of the rarest with only one to three percent of the populace displaying this character type.

What separates the INFJ is their capacity to take their vision and make an interpretation of it enthusiastically. They are not daydreamers or scholars who simply consider changing the world – they are equipped for taking their qualities and utilizing them to realize positive and enduring change.

While the MBTI is very prevalent, it has likewise been the wellspring of extensive analysis due to some degree to its poor legitimacy and dependability. In the event that you do take the MBTI, use alert when considering the importance of your results.1

You can study the INFJ character in this review, however this ought not be interpreted as wellbeing, mental, or expert vocation exhortation. INFJ is likewise something contrary to the ESTP character.

Key Characteristics Of Infj

With their solid feeling of instinct and passionate comprehension, INFJs can be mild-mannered and compassionate. This doesn't imply that they are push-over's, in any case. They have profoundly held convictions and a capacity to act conclusively so as to get what they need.

While they are thoughtful essentially, individuals with this character type can frame solid, important associations with other individuals. They appreciate helping other people, however they additionally need reality to revive.

While this character type might be portrayed by optimism, this doesn't imply that INFJs see only the good in everything. They comprehend the world, both the great and the awful, and want to have the option to improve it.

With regards to deciding, they place a more prominent accentuation on close to home worries than target actualities when deciding. They likewise prefer to apply control by arranging, sorting out and settling on choices as right on time as could reasonably be expected.

Qualities

- Delicate to the necessities of others

- Held

- Exceptionally imaginative and masterful

- Concentrated on what's to come

- Qualities close, profound connections

- Appreciates pondering the importance of life

- Optimistic

Innovative – Combining a striking creative mind with a solid feeling of sympathy, Advocates utilize their inventiveness to determine not specialized difficulties, however human ones. Individuals with the Advocate character type appreciate finding the ideal answer for somebody they care about. This quality makes them magnificent instructors and consultants.

Keen – Seeing through untrustworthiness and deceitful intentions, Advocates step past control and deals strategies and into a progressively fair dialog. Backer characters perceive how individuals and occasions are associated. They are then ready to utilize that understanding to concentrate on the business at hand.

Rousing and Convincing – Speaking in human terms, not specialized, Advocates have a liquid, motivational composition style that interests to the internal visionary in their group of spectators. Backers can even be amazingly great speakers, talking with warmth and energy. This is particularly valid in the event that they are glad for what they are representing.

Definitive – Advocates' innovativeness, knowledge, and motivation can really affect the world. This is on the grounds that they can finish on their thoughts with conviction, self control, and the arranging important to oversee complex tasks as far as possible. Individuals with the Advocate character type don't simply observe the way things should be; they follow up on those experiences.

Decided and Passionate – When Advocates come to accept that something is significant, they seek after that objective with a conviction and vitality that can find others napping. Backers will cause trouble on the off chance that they should. Not every person likes to see this, however their enthusiasm for their picked reason is an indistinguishable piece of the Advocate character.

Philanthropic – These qualities are utilized for good. Backers won't take part in any activities or elevate convictions just to profit themselves. They have solid convictions and take the activities that they do on the grounds that they are attempting to propel a thought that they really accept will improve the world a spot.

Shortcomings

- Can be excessively touchy

- Some of the time hard to become acquainted with

- Can have excessively elevated standards

- Difficult

- Aversions encounter

Touchy – When somebody difficulties or scrutinizes Advocates' standards or qualities, they are probably going to get an alarmingly solid reaction. Individuals with the Advocate character type are exceptionally helpless against analysis and strife. Scrutinizing their intentions is the snappiest route to their awful side.

Amazingly Private – Advocates will in general present themselves as the summit of a thought. This is mostly in light of the fact that they put stock in this thought, yet in addition since Advocates are amazingly private with regards to their own lives. They utilize this picture to shield themselves from having to really open up, even to dear companions. Believing another companion can be considerably additionally trying for Advocates.

Perfectionistic – Advocate characters are everything except characterized by their quest for standards. While this is a superb quality from multiple points of view, a perfect circumstance isn't constantly conceivable – in legislative issues, in business, in sentiment. Promoters, particularly Turbulent ones, again and again drop or disregard sound and gainful circumstances and connections, continually accepting there may be a superior alternative not far off.

Continuously Need to Have a Cause – Advocate characters get so got up to speed in their interests that any of the awkward assignments that separate them and their optimal vision is profoundly unwelcome. Supporters like to realize that they are stepping toward their objectives. In the event that standard undertakings feel like they are disrupting the general flow – or more awful yet, there is no objective by any means – they will feel eager and frustrated.

Can Burn Out Easily – Their enthusiasm, fretfulness for routine support, vision, and outrageous protection will in general leave Advocates with couple of alternatives for releasing pressure. Individuals with this character type are probably going to deplete themselves very soon on the off chance that they don't figure out how to offset their beliefs with the substances of everyday living.

Subjective Functions

The MBTI was initially made by Isabel Myers and her mom Katherine Briggs during the 1940s dependent on the speculations of Swiss psychoanalyst Carl Jung. Jung accepted that various mental procedures made up every individual's mental sort. He distinguished four key mental capacities: thinking, feeling, sensation, and instinct. Every one of these capacities at that point will in general be either ostensibly engaged (extraverted) or deep down centered (withdrawn).

MBTI advocates regularly use what they allude to as a useful stack when examining results. You can think about the diverse intellectual capacities as the fixings that go into making up a character type. The particular formula for each sort is constrained by how these various fixings consolidate and cooperate. The MBTI itself depends on two key figures that consolidate various approaches to give us the 16 distinct sorts. First is simply the capacities, and second is the various leveled request of those capacities.

Each type has a prevailing capacity that is the center normal for each kind. This is then bolstered by a helper work which is another well-created part of character. The tertiary and second rate capacities are less cognizant and not also framed.

INFJs will in general depend more on four essential psychological capacities:

Overwhelming: Introverted Intuition

This implies they will in general be profoundly centered around their inner experiences.

When they have framed an instinct about something, they will in general stick to it firmly, frequently to the point of being resolute in their core interest.

Along these lines, they are now and again seen as being obstinate and unwavering.

Helper: Extraverted Feeling

This normal for this sort makes INFJs profoundly mindful of what other individuals are feeling, however it implies they are some of the time less mindful of their own feelings.

INFJs some of the time battle to disapprove of other individuals' solicitations consequently. They are so sensitive to what other individuals are feeling that they dread causing dissatisfaction or hurt emotions.

Tertiary: Introverted Thinking

INFJs settle on choices dependent on thoughts and speculations that they structure dependent on their own bits of knowledge.

INFJs depend essentially on their thoughtful instinct and outgoing inclination when deciding, especially when they are around other individuals. At the point when they are distant from everyone else, in any case, individuals with this character type may depend more on their independent reasoning.

In distressing circumstances, an INFJ may attempt to depend on feelings when deciding, particularly in the event that it means satisfying other individuals. Under less unpleasant conditions, be that as it may, an INFJ is bound to depend more on their instinct.

Second rate: Extraverted Sensing

While this is a less created and to a great extent oblivious part of the INFJ, it has an effect on character.

This part of character enables the INFJ to focus on their general surroundings and remain mindful of their environment.

Outgoing detecting likewise helps INFJs better live right now, as opposed to just stressing over what's to come.

This part of character likewise helps INFJs acknowledge physical exercises, for example, climbing and moving.

Individual Relationships

INFJs likewise have an ability for language and are generally very great at conveying everything that needs to be conveyed. They have a distinctive inward life, however they are frequently reluctant to impart this to others aside from maybe those nearest to them. While they are calm and delicate, they can likewise be great pioneers. In any event, when they don't take on clear positions of authority, they regularly go about as calm influencers in the background.

INFJs are driven by their solid qualities and search out significance in all aspects of their lives including connections and work. Individuals with this kind of character are regularly portrayed as profound and complex. They might not have an immense hover of associates, however their dear kinships will in general be extremely close and dependable.

INFJs are keen on helping other people and improving the world a spot. They will in general be astounding audience members and are great at cooperating with individuals which whom they are sincerely close and associated. While they care profoundly about others, INFJs will in general be extremely independent and are just ready to share their "actual selves" with a chosen few. In the wake of being in social circumstances, INFJs need uninterrupted alone time to "energize."

Profession Paths

INFJs do well in professions where they can express their innovativeness. Since individuals with INFJ character have such profoundly held feelings and qualities, they do especially well in occupations that help these standards. INFJs frequently best in vocations that blend their requirement for imagination with their craving to roll out important improvements on the planet.

INFJs are generally high achievers and exceed expectations in scholastics and the working environment. They can be fussbudgets on occasion and will in general put a lot of exertion into their work. Colleagues will in general feel that INFJs are persevering, positive, and simple to coexist with. Since they are withdrawn, in any case, they may find that they have to withdraw on occasion to energize.

In administrative jobs, INFJs can here and there battle to apply authority. They will in general lead with affectability and are great at helping subordinates feel acknowledged in the working environment. Occupations that require a lot of routine or adherence to exacting guidelines can be troublesome or INFJs.

Tips for Interacting With INFJs-inclined people

Companionships

Since they are saved and private, INFJs can be hard to become more acquainted with. They place a high incentive on close, profound connections and can be harmed effectively, despite the fact that they regularly conceal these emotions from others. Collaborating with an INFJ includes understanding and supporting their need to withdraw and revive. Individuals with this character type in some cases feel misjudged. You can be a decent companion by setting aside the effort to comprehend their point of view and valuing their qualities.

Child upbringing

Since INFJs are so talented at getting sentiments, they will in general be close and associated with their youngsters. They have exclusive requirements, and can have extremely high conduct desires. They are worried about bringing up youngsters that are benevolent, mindful, and humane. INFJs urge their youngsters to seek after their inclinations and gifts so as to completely understand their individual potential.

Connections

INFJs have an inborn capacity to comprehend other individuals' sentiments and appreciate being right up front, personal connections. They will in general prosper best in sentimental associations with individuals who they share their fundamental beliefs. As an accomplice, it is critical to give the help and enthusiastic closeness that an INFJ desires. Truthfulness, trustworthiness, and realness are for the most part characteristics that the INFJ acknowledges in their accomplice.

INFJ: Tips To Express Your Emotions – Therapist View

The loner's method for communicating with the world is to unobtrusively investigate it, and the equivalent goes for our inner world. We're continually having existential exchanges in our minds, contemplating life's importance, thus significantly more.

This is valid for certain character types, particularly the INFJ. The wheels are continually turning in our cerebrum, which can be debilitating however typically fulfilling. Alongside existential musings come an investigation of how we're feeling and why. INFJs are about the "why."

We infrequently let ourselves experience a feeling without attempting to make sense of why we are feeling that feeling — and a similar procedure happens as we attempt to make sense of how other individuals are feeling, as well.

It's no big surprise INFJs are known as the "advisor" type. We frantically need to know the inward activities of ourselves and our kin (and truly, even irregular outsiders, similar to the individual filtering our staple goods). We're very on top of how others are feeling, and if negative emotions are being felt, we need to know why — so we can take care of business.

Thus, INFJs are constantly prepared to go about as criminologists so as to make sense of why a friend or family member is feeling blue. At that point we will take a wide margin to enable them to feel good. We request feelings. We ask for them to be conveyed to us. What's more, when all is said in done, individuals are hugely appreciative to have a sounding board for them to ricochet their feelings off of.

Chapter 6 Tricks to focus the mind

Stubborn body language refers to how an individual stands, sits, move, reacts, and appears to someone else. Many people have heard of the culture of their bodies. I know a few that make it out to be ridiculous, unimportant, and time-lost. That's not real. But even with doubters, it's worth considering how you present yourself to employers and co-workers in these harsh economic times in general. If you want to know more about stubborn body language signals, you're interested in this chapter. Write on... Read on...

Most of the people we read on their bodily habits are stubborn. Hard to change. Therefore, it is probably a good idea to consider that you prepare, particularly when looking for a job.

Here are four tips on what people are interested in what they write. This is important for you to sit in front of a potential employer, as you want to use your body to show that you are not just interested in the company, but are interested in hearing everything about it.

1. Hold the eye in contact at all times, but at least 60%-75% of the time. Experts agree that when someone talks, he must maintain eye contact, but not listen to the other man.

2. Listening isn't everything. Using[literally] your face. Make sure you listen closely to what a hiring manager says. Nod, you are going as if to sign the full agreement. No overdoing]

3. Even if you sit in a chair, point to the job interviewer. It supports the remainder of your body.

4. Some know a smile. Many know a smile. But don't smile like the cat of Cheshire. Don't make the smile look fake.A genuine smile is always accepted and says,' I like you and what you do.' This is always a good result in interviews for a new job.

You tell and sell, or thwart your efforts, by how you position yourself. Check out the next four tips.

5. This is a well-known language, which could be a bit stubborn when trying to change it. It is so well known that if you are looking for a job, consider whether you have this habit that could impede your quest for jobs.

Number 5 on your stubborn body language chart addresses whether you're standing or sitting around your legs. Since this is a gesture well-known even for those who have not learned signals of body language, you don't want to cross your legs. This is often seen as a defensive language of the body. Place your hands on your lap or rest them casually on the arms of your chair. You can easily gesture hands to support what you say and respond nicely to what the interviewer says, by putting your arms into an open position. Seeing free, you're open to anything. All right to go?

6. Here are some real nasty habits, which some people don't even know they have. Such four beauties are described as humorous in films. In most social situations, they reflect poorly

on you, but especially in a job interview. (1) Tap your fingers on the desk (2) Mix your feet on walking (3) Bit your fingernails, and then (4) Playing with a pencil during an interview. Disgusting! Perception is what the language of the body relates to. It concerns your listening ability and things like your arm placement. But it's about how you behave, too. Can you project a sense of trust? Or do you behave with the wrong attitude... As if you own the world? Figure it out prior to your next job interview]

7. Act confident. Employment managers are employees. Most of the people who apply for a position are probably nervous. If you know that you are qualified for a job, nervousness could demonstrate to the hiring manager that this job is important to you[this is why you're a little nervous]. Don't overcompensate. Don't act like this is a no-big-deal interview. Avoid looking happy like it doesn't matter. Not good.

8. More than the credentials, a job interview. It is reasonable to assume that your curriculum vitae is sent and chosen for an interview because it meets the needs of the company for the place to open.

A good worker is more than skills. Employers are looking for employees consistent with other employees. You heard it. Are you a team player? Will you be a business asset? If that is the case, how? Would you mean that you are a troublemaker? Would you feel like the company owes you something after and during work? Know the answers prior to the interview because your body reflects your attitude] The last two tips are questions that usually are not directly answerable. The interviewer also relies on the language of the body to believe it.

9. It's another invitation to contact. Make sure you don't make unnecessary touch movements with harassment at the workplace — no back, arm, or thigh tap. In fact, there is no need for any excuse to contact anyone at work.

10. The exception, of course, is the handshake. This is a major social practice. It is accepted. In this case, it's all right to touch. But even a handshake has rules about body language. Normally, don't give an interviewer your hand until she first offers it. Don't hold it too long. Make your handshake strong, but don't take on debt collection like Mafiosos. Solid, fast, and professional.

Reduce your aggressive body language patterns. Practice. Practice. Practice. Practice. Practice. Each time you visit a potential employer, you will consider that their body language tells you the right story.

The Body Language Is The Ultimate Language For Sex

Albert Mehrabian is a retired UCLA professor of psychology. He is renowned for his research on body language and particularly for the creation of approximate percentages of verbal and nonverbal interaction. His study assessed how, when people expressed likes and dislikes, they conveyed the true story through their expressions, body language, and voice tone. He concluded that words represent just 7% of the message, while voice toning accounted for 38% and body language for 55%. So if the body tells 55% of the story in terms of loves and dislikes, it matters when it comes to sex.

The key to good sex life and of a better life, in general, is that: places, sex toys, or "new" experiences will enhance sex if we have not acquired the main and most robust ability any person can have to listen and respond effectively. This ability is particularly tricky between the two genders because men look and react to different parts of their brains than women. The fact that we use different parts of our minds to interact is perfectly natural and thus crucial in good sex life.

The last term we are taught is that we listen with our eyes in kindergarten. This is not the case-our ears absorb sound waves. However, our minds listen. Furthermore, we also receive signals from our eyes when we take account of body language. They don't just see the language of the body when it comes to sex; they also feel signals, hear signals, smell signals, and taste signals. Gender is the primary contact medium. The whole body tells a story that blends smells, tastes, emotions, and sounds with pleasure.

But, the thing about Gender is because our whole body talks, it fully represents our brain. We can not separate our minds from our bodies, especially if we give ourselves so entirely. This is precisely where the trap happens-all of our worries, inhibitions, and doubts, together with our hopes, are expressed.

This is the key to understanding sex: fear stops us; freedom enables us to experience more. Therefore, to have better sex, we must be able to interact!

We can all use the same words and build sentences roughly in the same way, but every human being has their language. As babies, we responded to the touch of our mother. As children, through our personal experiences, we learned the meaning of words. We have developed a more profound value for these words as young people, and as adults, we use them to be productive. Our language understanding is so different in our experiences that each one of us has a unique language. What we do is a miracle–especially our survival needs to override the possible conflicts of the misunderstandings that we regularly have.

I grew up when "Women's Lib" exploded-as a boy we had been told that men should listen to women, but since no man knew exactly what that meant in my previous generation, we were not of good self-esteem when it came to girls. We felt insufficient to understand and listen to them because we somehow couldn't make an impression with all our efforts. Only when we met a girl who didn't expect me to know everything in advance did we think.

After many years of kind ties and many personal encounters, we found a simple way to learn the language of a woman: inquire. When you do something new with your hands, hear her breathing, feel her body's response, hear the sounds she makes-when they tell you all that it's right, it may be suitable. However, girls make the same noises during sex while excavating dishwashing fluid under the sink, and we men are baffled. Instead of trying to figure out whether "oh my god, do it again" is grumbling or "that isn't it!" ask if what you're doing works for her. If it does, proceed. If not, ask her to move your hand or try something new. You will soon learn what sounds and body movements are like a good time and what is like pain.

To be able to ask demonstrates a lot of maturity and confidence—these are two qualities that are very common and relate to the entire sex experience. Using this discovery approach, we would learn very quickly what the girl likes or dislikes, and by doing what works, we can ask for some of the best experiences.

The threat of revealing oneself gender is just like a blessing as it is a curse as the ultimate form of communication. Many people are naturally aware of this and try to manage the risk of exposure too overtly by maintaining and over-stressing those places when it comes to sex. Sex is not at its best if you can't give or receive all. So it takes time to learn the secret language she uses to reveal herself. Don't expect great sex in one night, sometimes good sex, but if that was better, imagine what it would be if you knew her!

The reluctance that we have to open up so fully can be very healthy. This helps us to restrict our emotional engagement and gives us time to make sure we have chosen the right partner. That is why gender is improving in long-term relationships (assuming that the partners work on it). However, in some cases, children's experiences, social norms, or beliefs can sexually inhibit us in an unhealthy way. As the person in the relationship, this is your task, overcome these fears and inhibitions to release your partner's passion.

This is precisely what the story is all about—the further we understand someone, the better the sex. The ancient Hebrew word for sex in the Bible means "to know." It is not whether you believe in the Bible is irrelevant; an ancient culture has understood that sex is equal to knowledge. Knowing her is the key to unlocking your passion.

Body Language That Sabotages Your Achievem ent

The language of the body communicates a lot to others around us. Much of my body language may be subconscious rather than aware, and some of our nonverbal signals may contradict what we want to communicate through gestures, facial expressions, and other messages. The non-verbal communication and indications we give without realizing it is most perplexing. If we don't know, that our effectiveness or influence can be restricted, how can we rectify it?

Raising awareness of such messages could make sure that our non-verbal communication doesn't really destroy what we say by choosing our words. The first step is to increase the awareness of some of the non-verbal signals, especially with regard to body language and their impact. Only then can we see if we actually show these features and try to create new habits overtime if necessary.

Gestures, people interpret how we hold our bodies, our "body language." If anyone slouches, they often seem to try and look small, and others interpret this as a lack of trust or conviction, or even that the person is insignificant. On the other hand, someone who stands or occupies more room seems dominant, confident, and responsible.

This comparison is especially important for women who learn that a small woman (thin, small, etc.) is more desirable. We are not taught to seem bigger than we are, but the message was more likely to appear smaller.

Another style comparison that doesn't always help people is that we have been taught to cross our legs, historically to indicate that they are restrained, feminine, and perhaps to show our legs. Any gesture that involves the protection of the central section (think underbelly), however, reflects weakness or discomfort. The crossing of the arms or legs may be seen as defensive or as weaker than the other person.

Pay attention to your shoulders, arms, and legs, and see what they say on you the next time you meet. Do they convey a relaxed trust or something closer to defensiveness? Practice then to change your posture and body language before you enter the room and notice any differences in how others accept and perceive you.

Facial Expressions could give away a lot about what we think, even if we don't think we have changed anything. Examples include interest, skepticism, boredom, frustration, embarrassment, and much more. Much is communicated to people with us.

The aim of this observation is not to try to hide your expressions— an attempt to mask guilt is often demonstrated in an effort to have an expressionless face, possibly combined with an avoidance of eye contact. It may, therefore, be unintended and more damaging to try to control your facial expressions, as someone else may perceive you as deceitful!

But if we know how much we give in our terms, we can at least try to minimize the impact. For example, if we're angry but don't want the other person to be angry or to defend, we can try to relax our mouth and brow to ease expression while explaining our point of view.

Cool factor Stress can affect how many ways we see ourselves. You can miss some minor nuances of your aspect when you're buried and rush through tasks (a stray hair, a button you forgot to do, etc.). When you are worried or under stress, facial tension, raised shoulders, and our facial expressions can be present.

Women tend to play with their hair in particular. This gesture is often self-soothing, but it can also give the unconscious message that the person is worried or uncomfortable because of it. Similar gestures could also include neck rubbing, hand massage, or an earlobe holding.

When the person around us looks calm, cool, and collected, but we show signs of stress, it diminishes our impact on the situation and lowers our ability to influence. Notice and proactively manage stressors and fatigue and take some time to calm down and focus before an important meeting.

For many years, Mirroring Salespersons have known that if they act very differently from you, it is harder to establish a relationship and therefore sell. But if you adjust your speech, gestures, and body language to match your own, you will unconsciously relax and sense a connection. The result is that you give the impression that you are "on the same page," or more like the person you are talking with.

You know, when others use the mirroring technique and its effect, mirroring can be an effective communication tool that can help you build a relationship and influence others. However, there is a good line between doing this efficiently and just appearing as a creepy cat, so exercise restraint and judgment when exercising this strategy, or it could turn it around.

Image and style as far as body language is not exactly concerned, how we dress can affect our non-verbal communication and how we are perceived as well. Although we would like to think that external factors do not affect people's views on our abilities, they do, sadly. When you're dressed like a summer intern, it will make you feel different than when you're dressed as an upcoming manager. If creativity is one of your strengths, but your clothes are conservative and stuffy, it will be harder for others to recognize your creative brilliance.

In some fields of this chapter, it really is easier to keep awareness and modify our behavior while others are deep-seated and subconscious. Some of them are clearer about what we have to do to change our perceptions. And in some areas, each person can be strong and face challenges. But we all have moments in life and in business in which we wonder, "I wasn't clear? How could I be misunderstood?" Perhaps we can use them as opportunities to look at our non-verbal communication in greater detail to see if we unconsciously sabotage our message.

Chapter 7 Types of communication

Intrapersonal Communication

The communication that happens within us, such as monologues or speaking to no one, constitutes intrapersonal communication. For instance, when you interrogate yourself loudly or assure yourself loudly, "I can," then this is intrapersonal verbal communication. Intrapersonal verbal communication can also happen where you scream at yourself, "Boy, I am a letdown; why?" In intrapersonal verbal communication, one is fully aware that they are speaking to the inner self and voice it. Intrapersonal verbal communication is different from speaking to an inanimate object. Most people speak to themselves but do not verbalize it.

Interpersonal Communication

It is a form of communication that happens between two individuals. For instance, when you are talking to a classmate, you are engaging in interpersonal communication. In interpersonal communication, emotional intelligence is important as the communicators need assurance that the other person is listening and understanding as well as relating to the message. Interpersonal communication is relative communication as it requires adjusting the communication to accommodate the other person. The participants frequently switch between the sender and receiver roles. When done physically, most of the interpersonal communication happens within close distance.

Small Group Communication

It is communication involving more than two people and but less than a large gathering. In simple terms, the audience does not require the speaker to shout or use a public address system. In group communication, many of the participants are allowed to interact and mingle with the rest. The participants take turns to speak and may interrupt the conversation at any point. A small group communication requires social skills such as leadership, conflict management, and cultural competence to make everyone feel comfortable and appreciated.

For instance, through persuasion and influencing skills, one will find public social space not only approachable but fulfilling. The art of showing enthusiasm in other individuals and convincing them to buy into your ideas is known as persuasion. Persuasive or influential people will read the emotional currents in a situation and perfect what they are saying to appeal to spur involved. Persuasion is a function of communication and personality and this demands that you become an effective communicator who is empathetic to others. Winning over people requires trying to convince them to join your course. One must learn to sell your views as a salesperson would do.

As indicated, leadership is critical in all aspects of social interactions and in resolving conflicts. Against this backdrop, emotional intelligence and leadership skills are connected in multiple ways. The ability to influence requires that you tune your emotions and those of others to win them over. Influence is a critical attribute of good leadership. It is sometimes called charisma but though leadership skills involving influence go beyond charisma to align with good emotional intelligence. The competencies of good leadership require you to articulate a vision and those other people with it. One does not have to be in a formal leadership position to exhibit leadership. While holding your colleagues accountable, support and direct their performance. Aspire to learn to lead by example.

Public Communication

When one addresses a large gathering of people, it becomes public communication. Public communication requires preparation and research on the demographics of the audience. Expectedly, cultural competence is important as audiences are diverse and sensitive to religious affiliation, ethnicity, sexual orientation, and gender. Public communication requires formal language and explicit use of transitional phrases to help the audience connect. The language used in communication should be free of jargon.

How Nonverbal Communication is Related to Body Language

In this context, nonverbal communication refers to body language. Starting with facial expressions, the human face is highly expressive and conveys countless emotions even without verbalizing anything. Fortunately, nonverbal communications are standard as the facial expressions for happiness, anger, sadness, and fear are the same across cultures. Like most aspects of nonverbal communication, one has little control over the source and manifestation of facial expression, making it a critical aspect of evaluating the honesty of communication. From facial expressions, we can determine how one is feeling.

Then there is body movement and posture. How one stands, sits, holds their head or walks affects how one is perceived by others. For instance, our posture communicates much about our attentiveness and eagerness when listening to a speech. Our posture also communicates our emotional status. If one is angry, they are unlikely to appear composed, and they are likely to stand upright for long or slouch for long. When one is excited, he or she is likely to change posture and movements frequently than when one feels sad. Recall when you felt highly excited, you probably walked fast, jumped, sat, and stood up frequently than usual.

Another form of nonverbal communication is gestures. Hand gestures are used to beckon, wave, point, or direct. In most cases, hand gestures happen without much intervention from the conscious mind. The meaning of most hand gestures varies across cultures. An innocent message created by a hand gesture in one country may be offensive in another country. We can read the emotional status of an individual from their hand gestures even if they speak the contrary. For instance, when one is angry, he or she is likely to throw their hands in the air in an uncoordinated manner. In most instances, hand gestures contradict verbal communication, especially where one is feeling emotional and tries to mask it.

Correspondingly, there is eye contact, which is a critical component of body language. The way one looks at another person during communication indicates hostility, affection, interest, and confidence. Individuals that have difficulties initiating and sustaining eye contact are largely considered shy. When one feels embarrassed, he or she is likely not to make and sustain eye contact. Prolonged eye contact at a particular person or group of people is a stare and indicates judgment. Think of how your teacher looked at you when you were talking while others were writing. Prolonged eye contact is used to judge and intimidate.

Another critical aspect of body language is touch. A lot of meaning is attached to touch and in some cases, touch impacts the development of a person. In the formative years, children need touch, reassuring fondle to feel secure and loved. In fact, psychologists can determine bonding issues where one of the parents shows reluctance to touch and fondle their kid. For adults, touch manifests commonly as a handshake and a hug. A firm handshake denotes confidence and familiarity while a weak handshake suggests a lack of confidence and unfamiliarity. A hug serves the same role as a handshake but hugs for individuals in love may be prolonged.

Equally important there is space as part of nonverbal communication. Getting too close to the person you are having a conversation with will make them uncomfortable unless it is in exceptional situations. For lovers trying to connect more with each other, getting closer to each other may sound romantic. In teaching, there is what they call the professional distance which is the standard distance allowable between a teacher and the student when communicating. When someone gets too close then the other person may feel suffocated, trapped, and intimidated. Getting too far is also counterproductive as it makes the other person strain to participate in the communication.

Then there is a voice as part of nonverbal communication. How loud we speak denotes emphasis. The pace of our speaking captures our emotional status. Speaking fast may indicate that one has panicked or one is feeling insecure and wants to get through with speaking as fast as they can. The tone and inflection of the voice tell more about the attitude of the speaker and the nature of the message. For instance, the message may sound standard and devoid of emotions but the tone and pitch of the speaker may bring out excitement or temper. The tone of the speaker may indicate anger or sarcasm.

Even though nonverbal communication can be manipulated or faked, it is difficult to manipulate all forms of nonverbal communication in one episode. It is not possible to fake tone, gestures, touch, distance and facial expressions to align with verbal communication. For this reason, body language remains a strong source of reading and ascertaining the emotional status of an individual. Nevertheless, it is possible to learn and exert control over your body language to enhance particular outcomes. Just like we learn to guide our emotions and subsequent reactions, we can exert more control over body language. There is also a possibility of receiving confusing nonverbal communication, which is unintentionally sent by the source. In most cases, a confusing nonverbal communication harms relationships. At some point, you might have smiled unintentionally only for your friend to think you are celebrating their losses.

Chapter 8 Brain and body language perception

When someone say the word "boss," the first thing that pops into our heads is a superior, influential, and straightforward man or woman who, no matter how long you've been working with them, is still fearsome. A lot of us still have problems approaching our boss even after working with them for years. To be honest, talking to your boss isn't really that hard - all you need is confidence and sometimes a little wit.

Some employees tremble at the sight of their boss, and a lot are more worried in making a decision whether to approach their boss at all for fear that they might make the wrong move. Certainty is a very powerful tool here. If you can decipher your boss' mood and be certain of how he or she feels, then approaching your boss is not going to be a problem, and creating a positive image for yourself is going to be a piece of cake. Knowledge is power and if you can read what your boss is saying through recognition of key body language indicators, you'll be a step ahead of everyone else!

The Handshake

Always notice your boss' gestures and postures. When giving a handshake, bosses tend to give their hand with the palm facing down, making you accept it with the face of your palm facing up. Such a position eventually corresponds to you being submissive to him and him being superior to you. This however is very hard to reverse. Since superior people always compete for dominance and superiority, it would degrade their ego if they were the one to be submissive. So what do you do to make it even? What do you do to show that there's more to you than being just a typical, submissive employee? Next time, do a double grip: accept the handshake submissively but firmly, and then use your other hand to handicap his hand, hence giving him the idea that you're not a sheep, that you have the will and confidence of an equal, and you have the audacity to prove it.

Eye focus

The eyes say a lot about a person. Eyes are also an essential tool in body language. You can understand how a person feels through the direction in which their eyes are looking. This is also a good way to know how your conversation with the boss is going. If you're trying to be friendly with your boss and you notice that his eyes are somewhat glued to his watch or on his paperwork, change your strategy, because it's a cue that your boss isn't interested in your presence. Another situation is if by chance, you're chatting with your boss on the hallway, or on the elevator, and then you notice him looking at something else other than you, it's also a sign of distraction and disinterest. To say that a conversation is going well, you must see the other party looking at you with attentive eyes - a very common sign of interest.

Critical Evaluation and Hand-To-Face Gestures

The signal for a critical evaluation is the hand-to-face gesture. This position includes the index finger pointing up to the cheek with another finger covering the mouth and the thumb supporting the chin. Further proof that a person is having a critical evaluation is when the arms and legs are tightly crossed, giving away a defensive and negative non-verbal statement. The next time that you discuss a presentation with your boss and you see him or her in this posture, it's best to change your idea or politely dismiss yourself because when the boss says at the end "I'll think about it," what he or she is really saying is, "I don't like your presentation."

Mirroring

One of the biggest reasons that a lot of us fear our boss is how they make us feel inferior. To fight this, mirror the actions of your boss, but not mockingly or in a disrespectful way. Mirroring shows how close you are to a certain someone. Two friends who are very close tend to copy each other's postures involuntarily - smiling, clapping, and so on. It is not a requirement for you to be already close to a person in order to mirror him. In fact, faking it when talking to an acquaintance tends to develop your relationship in a better way. So if you want to be close to your boss, mirror his or her actions: stand up straight, speak up with power, and believe that you are equals.

Superiority

Don't you just hate it when you enter your boss' office, start talking about a meeting or a presentation, and then suddenly your boss clasps his or her hands and puts them behind their head? This gesture states superiority. What your boss is actually trying to say is rather like boasting. This gesture typically means, "Ha! I'm so much powerful than you" or even, "Yes, someday perhaps when you become smarter than I . . ." No wonder even without saying those words directly, the action in and of itself annoys you! Next time, when you see this sort of gesture, mirror it, only then will your boss think that something is wrong, and then he or she will break from this position. Their next gesture would probably be a crossed arm - one that suggests inner defense!

Always remember to look for group clusters before deciphering someone else's body language. When talking to your boss, here are some possible scenarios and body signals that you might have already encountered.

John is a very hardworking businessman. He worked at his company for five years. For the time being, he wanted to achieve a higher ranking, so he went into the boss' office to ask for a raise. The first thing he saw there was his boss, sitting in his high and comfy chair. John approached him quite trembling, and then sat on a chair next to the table. He doesn't know what to say. He crossed his arms and legs, and then he tapped anxiously on the folder he is currently holding - an obvious sign of nervousness and unpreparedness. The boss then asked him what he wanted, but John just kept on stuttering words and avoiding his boss' gaze. The room was filled with dead air for a while until the boss stopped, clasped his hands together, and put them behind his head. Then he looked at John and asked if he went in to ask for a raise. John's eyes lit up because the boss finally figured out his intention. He also felt embarrassed, thinking he might not meet the requirements. This attitude eventually destroys his confidence. When John was asked to show his company profile and achievements, he merely passed over a folder containing his documents and sat silently as he looked at the boss scanning through it. The boss then handed him back his files. He touched his nose, rubbed his eyes, and then he said, "John, I will think about it." Then he offered John a handshake, signaling the end of discussion.

What could have happened if the body language was acknowledged and the approach was different? Here is an alternate version of the scene:

John is a very hardworking businessman. He worked at his company for five years. During that time, he wanted to achieve a higher ranking, so he went into the boss' office to ask for a raise. The first thing he saw there was his boss, sitting on his high and comfy chair. He walked to the boss' chair with a smile on his face, greeted the boss, and complimented his tie, creating a short conversation. John now got the attention of his boss after they shared a good laugh. Then, without further ado,

John stated his business - to ask for a raise. The boss asked for his company profile and achievements. John gave the documents. After scanning the files, the boss asked him a few questions. With confidence, John answered them gracefully as he accordingly copied his boss' gestures. The boss now felt quite easy with this fellow as he stood and offered him a handshake. Then he said, "John, I will think about it." John gladly accepted the handshake, and left the office politely.

What were the simple body gestures observed? Didn't they create a different result?

Here is another situation:

Linda is a new employee, and she strives to build a good relationship with everyone around her workplace. One day, during lunch, she met the boss in the canteen hallway. Taking this as an opportunity, she approached, greeted the boss, and started a conversation. During their communication, Linda noticed her boss repeatedly looking at his watch. She knew what this meant, but she continued talking anyway. To make matters worse, Linda talked about a lot of things that didn't really interest her boss. He responded while looking at anyplace except her, an indication of disinterest and boredom. When Linda's coworker John approached, the boss used this as an opportunity and immediately excused himself.

Here is an alternate version of the scene:

Linda is a new employee, and she strives to build a good relationship with everyone around her workplace. One day, during lunch, she met the boss in the canteen hallway. Taking this opportunity, she approached, greeted the boss, and started a conversation. During their communication, Linda noticed her boss repeatedly looking at his watch. She knew what this meant and as soon as she saw this, she immediately changed the subject until they stumbled upon something they both had an interest in. Linda mirrored her boss during the chat, and her boss then felt comfortable and mirrored her unknowingly as well. When her coworker John approached, the boss then dismissed himself politely and asked to talk again some other time.

Remember that your boss likes being a boss, being superior and being competitive. Those are what build his or her image. In order to get on your boss's good side, you must balance being a good leader and a good follower. To submit too much will make your boss think that you're incompetent and unworthy of a promotion, or even the job. But to leading too much will make him or her think of you as competition for their own position, which may lead to you getting fired! You can't really say "Sir, I'm trying to prove my worth in this company but I am not trying to steal your position," can you? The best way to deliver this message then is through body language. If you can understand all of what your boss is trying to say, verbally and non-verbally, then it will be easier for you to create a lighter and friendlier atmosphere every time the two of you talk.

Chapter 9 Body language and hidden meaning

This is crucial information to know for learning body language, but really it's just the vocabulary of the body. To understand any language you also need to understand grammar and syntax: how the words come together to form meaning.

To really understand and use body language you have to learn how to read it in action and how to view it holistically as an overall picture what a person is trying to communicate. If you want to begin controlling your own body language you'll have to understand how it all works together in the field as well. Somebody crossing their legs away from you could mean they are shy, it could mean that they are closed off to you, or it could just mean they need to pee desperately. To really be able to read what they are feeling you need to notice how they use the space around them, group behavioral actions into clusters (clusters are multiple body language cues placed together, so if they cross their legs away from you, cross their hands, and face in a direction away from you, it isn't looking good!), and to place them into context.

Actively Listening

If you are looking at somebody's posture or trying to pick up the micro-expressions in their face that occur at one-fifth of a second you might be closer to understanding how they really feel, but you might also be ignoring something more obvious. The whole point of studying body language is to better understand what people are really thinking so you can build a better connection to them. The point isn't to make you paranoid that they are constantly deceiving you. It's actually to make you less paranoid about what they are really thinking.

One of common reason people turn to body language is because they want to be more successful when it comes to meeting new people. They want to know if the person of their desire would like to go on a date. They are looking for ways to determine whether the other person likes them, or if they are having a good time. Then they want to know ways to effectively ensure the other person is having a good time. Before you get started spotting their body language, first listen to what they are saying, and how they are saying it. If somebody is asking questions about you and willingly talking to you this is a good sign they are interested in you. Typically we do not spend too much time or effort on people we don't want to be around.

You might have to ask yourself whether this person is providing small talk, but you can often distinguish between the two by assessing whether they are trying to actually learn more about you. Small talk is an instrument of social politeness that is not really intended to establish much of a deeper connection and is centered around surface topics and subjects. Ask yourself, would you be putting forward the questions they are asking if you just wanted to make small talk?

Make sure to look for specific tells that a person is interested in you. Are they laughing overly enthusiastically at what you are saying? Are they trying to keep the conversation going? Are they trying to find shared interests or shared experiences? Are they complementing you? Do they keep hinting at the idea of spending more time together in the near future? Do they physically touch you as they talk, and are they keeping strong eye contact or providing any tells of shyness? If you can determine what someone wants clearly from what they are saying, then connecting the pieces together with body language is a much easier task. This doesn't just apply to dating but any social interaction.

Being Sherlock Holmes...

Before we move on, there is another important step in reading what someone has to say – which is asking why. The most important thing to answer is why is this person talking to me? In some circumstances this is going to be very obvious. If you walk into McDonald's and the person behind the counter asks for your order there is no mystery about why they spoke to you. Try to take things deeper than just superficial reasons though. Why did your boss call on you specifically to be in this meeting? Why is the person on the bus striking up a conversation with you when they could be reading a book? You can take this further and consider why someone would ask you a specific question. Do they value your opinion? Are they testing you? Do they really want to ask you something else?

Lastly, try to recall any background information you have about a person. If you know someone is single that will help you determine if they are flirting with you. If they told you they were bored you might be able to determine they are attempting to entertain themselves. If they are about to give a big speech you can read a closed off body as nerves rather than annoyance. Taking the time to look for the most obvious or unsaid parts of a conversation can save you a lot of energy. Don't look for the subtleties before you've heard what someone has actually said and placed it into context.

Proxemics

Proxemics is a fancy word used in the body language community to mean the study of personal space and proximity. You can't truly read someone's body language without noticing where they are in relation to you in space.

Someone seems to be paying attention to you, they have open body language, they are even pointing themselves towards you – so they're clearly paying attention to you right? Well, maybe not if they're on the other side of the room and not moving any closer towards you.

In general, intimate space is up to the range of 1 foot away from you (close enough to touch or whisper), personal space is between 1 and 4 foot from you (mostly used by close friends or family), social space is between 4 and 12 foot (speaking to a colleague about work), and public space is between 12 and 25 foot (you would have to speak in a loud voice to get someone's attention).

Humans are innately conscious of their personal space and feel uncomfortable when it's encroached upon. To such an extent that people who have experienced certain types of brain damage (specifically to the amygdale) will struggle to maintain a socially appropriate level of distance. The amount of distance that is considered acceptable varies a lot from country to country as well as individual to individual. Often countries that are quite small in size or very densely populated such as Japan have smaller realms of personal space than the typical American will have.

When it comes to reading other people, certain elements of personal space are obvious. If someone is close it will mean they are, or are trying to be, more intimate. However, with some people, especially men, there is a tendency to be territorial and to feel they have more access to your personal space than you might feel comfortable with. You can use these cues to determine if someone is being aggressive, friendly, or flirtatious. By reading the rest of someone's body language you can see if they are leaning towards you to be friendly or to be assertive. It is quite risky to try and invade other people's personal space to get an advantage over them so in general try to avoid getting too close to someone unless they invite you to by touching you or speaking at a lower volume that requires you to lean in.

The US President Lyndon B. Johnson is famous for his use of body language and there are many images online of him using his body language by leaning towards people to force them to take a more defensive stance. It's a powerful move but also an aggressive one that may not make you the most popular person in the room. If you are trying to get a point across or stay firm in what you are saying however, it is a useful move to make. Parents often use this on their children when they are in trouble.

Behavioral Clusters

Body language rarely occurs in just one individual body part, so you can't simply read each part of the body in isolation. In the body language community people's moods are often said to be telegraphed in clusters of behavioral actions (body language) that come together to show you the bigger picture.

There are said to be six universal visual signals: happiness, sadness, surprise, disgust, anger, and fear. In general it's not overly difficult to tell the difference between positive and negative signals or emotions. We generally know if someone is down about something – we just can't always be sure if they are annoyed, nervous, or sad. Individually, body parts won't always help because a lot of these moods can be hidden by avoiding eye contact, and becoming more closed off with their body language. There can even sometimes be confusion between, for example, someone that is being submissive and nervous because they like you, or being submissive and nervous because they fear you.

Listening to your gut is very important here. Even though you may not have been consciously picking up on these things when communicating with others, you would be quite well trained to know whether someone is taking a big open posture to be aggressive or to be friendly. Look to see whether their behavior is congruent with the situation you are in and what they have been saying. If a person's body language has changed a lot after you made a comment about someone's appearance you can read whether they are pleased or irritated.

To start reading behavioral clusters better you have to start looking for general patterns. If they are sitting further away from you, if they are turned away from you, if they are closed up, if they are not making eye contact, or otherwise blocking you off then they it is likely they could be upset – almost certainly with you if this is unusual behavior on their behalf. From this example what you would have noticed is a general pattern of them turning away from you in every aspect of their body.

You need to be able to make fairly quick snap-judgments about other people, so you need to group different behaviors and movements together to determine certain things. This is termed as relying on heuristics, which is a quick way of problem-solving and a mental shortcut to decision-making when our minds have to figure things out with minimal information available and limited time. Are they being dominant or submissive? Are they being aggressive or defensive? Are they being open or closed? Are they relaxed or tense? Are they interested or uninterested?

The skill of reading clusters is more useful in environments where people try to hide their feelings and when you are looking to have some kind of success. This is usually at work or in the dating scene. To get better at reading clusters you will have to piece together the small clues and take a guess then see if you turn out to be correct in your assessment. When you are confident about the way someone is feeling, make a note of how their body language comes together so you can use it for future reference (this is called a baseline and will be discussed shortly). You can easily practice this by people watching as you go about your daily life, it is generally obvious how people are feeling or communicating when they are in small groups.

When you are dealing with liars, sales people or people attempting to be disingenuous or deceptive, you may have increased difficulty in determining what their body is saying. Your best option is to look to context and use good detective work; it's usually easiest to see if someone is lying by discovering whether their story adds up. If you are doubtful you can then see if their body language suggests they are being anxious or taking a while to respond. Conversation is usually instantaneous; taking extra time to reply is one of the more useful indicators that someone is being dishonest. Although taking longer to respond on its own is not a guarantee someone is lying as all people vary in how quickly they respond in conversation. This is where baselines come into effect and is covered in the next heading.

When it comes to sales people or general con artists you have to see whether their body language is appropriate to the situation you find yourself in. Is someone you just met being overly friendly as if they are trying to lead you somewhere? Is what they are saying matching what they are doing with their body?

Through practice you will start to see pick up on clusters consistently, but just a little practice will make you far more confident. Take the time to people watch and observe others the next time you are out and about and make a mental profile of other people's behavior and clusters. By reading other people better and discovering general profiles and patterns, you can then attempt to adopt them for yourself and become more confident in your dealings with other people.

It All Comes Down To The Bottom Baseline

When it comes to reading body language it often feels like you are being trained to always work with strangers and to speak some universal language. But the truth is that everyone is different and has an individual way of speaking. When reading other people you will likely be reading a few of the same people a lot, so you need to start developing a baseline level for how they behave. If you know what normal body language is for them, then you can determine when things are out of place. This is what is known as a baseline. Every environment and person has a baseline. A baseline is simply what's normal in a given situation, and it differs for individuals as it does for environments. For example, the baseline at a library will usually involve people reading a book, working on their laptops or the library computers, or looking for a book to read on the shelves. The baseline at a rock concert would be loud booming music and people looking at the stage while dancing like mad man. If you switched it around and had someone dancing around like a mad man at a library, and someone in the crowd of a rock concert reading a book, the person would look really out of place.

The point of baselines is to use them as a reference point so that we can notice when things are out of place when it comes to someone's body language. If someone generally carries themselves upright and is smiling but today they are slouched and neutral faced, you will know something is bothering them. On the other hand, if someone is slouched and neutral faced all the time, oh you know "That's just how they are". This is why body language isn't the best tool to rely on when first meeting someone as you don't know what their baseline is. It may just be that they always drag their feet when they're walking or that they talk at a surprisingly fast speed even though they aren't excited. Start working on establishing baselines for close friends and family. First take note of what emotion or feeling they may be expressing and then take a mental picture of their body language to use as a baseline in the future.

Chapter 10 Not verbal communication

Putting People At Ease

When someone greets you with a smile, it's polite to smile back at them. The smile is an unspoken gesture that helps put people at ease. When we smile, we're announcing that we are not a threat to anyone. To smile yourself, or to see someone else smile at you, helps to release those feel-good hormones of endorphins and serotonin. That, in turn, helps to lower blood pressure, so it's a very healthy gesture to perform or to receive. It is certainly one of those gestures that does not require words and is very infectious.

When someone smiles at you and you return it, by mirroring their gesture you are showing them that you understand how they feel. You are also indicating that you feel the same way. This is only one small example of how we use nonverbal gestures to communicate with one another. It's not something we do intentionally. When we mirror a smile in the right situation it helps to build up trust. Each understands that both are on the same wavelength. In turn, they will feel they can have a rapport with one another.

A study in 2017 indicated that women tend to smile more than men. (22), Men are more likely to express annoyance in their facial expressions. It showed that men prefer to mirror other body gestures that don't involve the face so much.

Synchronization In Romance

Romantic relationships often involve two people who are in rapport with one another. When sexually attracted they may not realize how much they mimic each other's actions. A woman may twirl hair through her fingers. She is in an excited, yet anxious, moment as she speaks with a man she feels attracted to. In response, the man may pull at his ear, or run his fingers through his hair. He is fidgeting with his fingers as he mirrors her actions. Subconsciously, he's observing her every move. These two people are in-tune with one another.

Mirroring someone in a conversation is a form of micro-gestures. They help to put people in sync with one another. It can be seen happening in many parts of the body, such as:

- Blinking at the same time.

- Raising eyebrows at one another.

- The Crossing of arms or legs.

The Trust Of A Friend

Friends and loved ones tend to mirror one another's body movements the most. They have no hang-ups with each other's presence. That's because they've learned to trust each other over the years. But, they're not the only ones that do mirroring naturally.

Seeking A Promotion

Let's take those who are looking to move up the corporate ladder. In their keenness to impress the boss, they'll most likely inadvertently mirror the body movements of their superiors. They want to get the message across that they have similar points of view and respect the person they're mirroring. By subtly mimicking them, they are showing that they're in sync with them. These are the lengths many will go to for that hard-earned promotion.

Done wrong and it won't impress. Their actions may become misinterpreted as questioning their boss's leadership skills. Their boss may think that they believe they can do a better job. Instead, it may be seen as an invasive communication method. If mirroring is done in an over-obvious manner, then they can kiss that promotion goodbye! Or, if they happen to mimic their boss's negative movements, such as if they lick their lips a lot, they will soon be out of favor. The boss might read this as a fun-poking process and feel offended. It's a fine line to walk.

Group Influences

If you want to influence someone in a group to agree with your point of view or new idea, watch out for who's doing the mirroring and who is being mirrored. That way you are identifying who has the authority to agree with you. The one being mirrored is clearly a person of interest.

If you can show that you feel confident through your body language to a room full of people, you will build up confidence in those around you. Those that can do this, often find themselves as the natural leader of any group. Though if you enter the room yawning and rubbing your eyes, you're more likely to put your audience to sleep.

You can tell from the body language of your audience whether they agree or disagree with what you are trying to convey. Those in disagreement may act a little differently to everyone else. They will look like the odd one out if you learn what signs to look for. Though you might need to focus, if they're good at it too, it may be very subtle.

We only tend to mirror each other when in conversation with people we know. It's unlikely we will mirror the behavior of complete strangers. It would not seem normal to mimic the person stood next to you in a queue for the cinema. Nor would we mimic people we're not very impressed with. It appears that mirroring has a hierarchy. Mimicking another's body language is a powerful tool for nonverbal communication. Not only can it help with that promotion, but it can also reveal whether someone has romantic intentions.

Dress Code Language

The messages you give away are not only through the use of your body language. Another form of nonverbal secrets can be how we wear and use our clothing and accessories. Our clothes are a part of our body, a kind of outer skin. There are few people who consider walking around naked to be the norm. Nor would we wear our pajamas to go to work or a business suit to bed.

We have discussed how the first few seconds of meeting someone can often be crucial to how we perceive them. For a part of that critical assessment, we will also be considering their visual presentation. Our judgment will include how a person looks, as well as how they move. We do all that before they mutter a single word.

It all comes back to that tiny window of our first impression. If we want to impress someone, we must wear what makes us feel good. When we dress up to go on a special night out, we can feel like we're walking on air. It's not only about attraction, but it's also about our identity. Visual identity is yet another unwritten set of rules sending out a message about who we are. Our clothing and accessories can also give away our social status in life. We advertise how financially comfortable we are and show our cultural background. Even our age and sexual identity can be reflected in our choice of dress. The clothes on your back are a powerful tool in nonverbal communication.

To emphasize this, let's consider some different forms of dress:

- Loose ill-fitting clothes that appear grubby, may give off the impression that the person is lazy and maybe even unhygienic.

- In Western cultures, if a woman wears a low-cut neckline on a tight dress, it may give off the impression her out for fun and seeking a sexual encounter.

- A man in a suit could be a businessman, or someone attending a formal occasion.

- Yet, if he wore open-toed sandals with his business suit it would certainly draw attention. It would confuse, as no one would expect these two pieces of clothing to go together.

What we wear clearly sends out a strong message but so too does our grooming. Many of us are fixated on how we look. Women paint in eyebrows to look attractive. Men hate it when their hair begins to thin-out on their head as it advertises aging. Are we a vain species or is this all simply a part of our communication methods?

If we are interviewing for employment, we like to look the part and dress in formal wear. We're attempting to give off a good impression which may help us to be the successful candidate. Not only has that, dressing-up helped to boost our confidence. Our clothing is our identity costume.

If we want to show respect to others, then we usually dress according to the unwritten rules. If we don't follow those rules then we give off a message of being deviant.

Nonverbal movements can send different messages for different cultures, so too can our costume of clothing:

- In the Middle East, a woman may feel quite vulnerable if she does not wear a burqa. Though because it's a warm clime she could walk around barefoot and no one would give a second glance.

- Yet, if you were to walk around barefoot in a Western city, people would think you rather odd. Nor would a woman need to cover her head with a burqa.

Most of us are practical and want to feel comfortable, so we tend to wear the right style of clothing for the occasion. There's no denying that what you wear sends out a loud visual message. If you are going to wear flashy clothes, then you'd better have the demeanor to match or others may be suspicious of you. Many of us wear what we can afford to buy. So it seems a little unfair and judgmental that so much is read into what a person is wearing.

It's not only clothing but your accessories too, particularly for women. These are not necessary items of clothing so if you choose to wear them, think about what they say about you. Plus, the perfumes we use, the way we wear our hair, the list is endless on how others might judge us.

Think of it this way, if we all dressed identically, we would lose an important tool that helps us to assess one another. Life would be rather boring if we all had the same personality, and equally if we all wore the same clothes.

In reality, we shouldn't put so much weight behind what someone is wearing. We should take the time to learn more instead of brushing over the surface. When assessing new people, we should all be a little more patient and a little less judgmental.

How then can we decide if we can trust someone and welcome them, if not by first impressions?

Chapter 11 Charisma

Some people seemingly have the ability to walk into a room and instantly turn heads. They ooze in charisma and have everyone's attention even before they mutter a single word. These people seem to be born leaders, the alphas, or the top dogs.

One thing for certain, we are not born charismatic so it must be something we can all learn to do.

One standout attribute of those who are charismatic is that they exude confidence. Their body language will play an important role in maintaining that popularity. Having an open and approachable body stance plays a key role in being popular and making friends. Your openness should invite friendliness but not display weakness. Though we all have weaknesses, we must learn to hide them well. Essentially, that smile you show off must look authentic and not false.

A charismatic person is always a good listener, or at least they should look as though they are. It's all about a pleasant attitude and giving substance and value to your words and movements. Inspiring others and compelling them to act. Remember, nonverbal movements reflect emotional moods. If you keep your head clear and focus on the show of confident words and movements, you should at least look the part.

Not everyone has that natural feeling of warmth towards other people. But you can learn how to feel relaxed when in other people's company. Focus on the other people and take your mind away from your own emotions. Get your mind in sync with your body movements. If you have practiced relaxation techniques, this will shine through in your attitude and movement.

It's much like the natural smile that releases endorphins. Stand tall and you will feel tall.

If you see someone slouching in a chair, what is your first impression of them? You're likely to sweep your eyes right past them because they make no significant impact upon you. You may even think they're drunk or tired and so not worth any attention.

Try to treat everyone as though you are about to make them your personal friend. What then is the right way to go about making friends?

Friendships And Acquaintances

It isn't easy to make someone so at ease that they feel like they've known you a lifetime. Having the skill to do that though will no doubt foster new friendships. The important point is that it is not words alone that help you achieve this but your reactions.

They are already subconsciously scanning your body language. Now's the time be making that first impression count. Although we know we should not judge with so little information at hand, the fact is that we do. It isn't a conscious decision as we do it without even thinking about it. If you want to learn better communication skills, then make it your new life goal to do gestures consciously. Greet strangers with a warm smile. Make it a genuine one so that it reflects through your eyes and facial muscles.

Oculesics - Eye Contact

Grab their attention with eye to eye contact. The average time we look at each other is only a mere 10-seconds, so make the most of it. Maintaining eye contact, even if the other looks away, is vital to allow your own confidence to shine through. Though tread carefully and don't overdo it. That could be seen as a challenge, which wouldn't get your first meeting off to a good start.

As you introduce yourself, observe how they are reacting. For example, if they don't maintain eye contact, it may imply they lack confidence themselves. It's up to you to make them feel comfortable and therefore more confident in your company.

Haptics – The Power Of Touch

If you must share a handshake, take their whole hand in a firm grasp. Don't act as if you think they have some disease and you don't wish to touch them for too long. Wait until they let go, allowing them to take the lead. Of course, don't make it so firm that it's seen as aggressive. Shaking their arm out of their socket will not achieve the positive reaction you seek.

Try a handshake with both hands if they appear to be nervous or lacking in confidence. Gently place your other hand on top of theirs, completely encompassing it.

This type of touch-communication is known as Haptics. It is often reserved for those you love and trust. What you are doing is showing them that you are not afraid to do something out of the ordinary. Especially if it means you can help them to feel more at ease. If done in the correct manner, you will come across as warm and open-minded.

Listen And Mirror

To understand another's movements, it's wise to keep your own nonverbal actions open, wide open. Listen to their words and observe their movements closely. Only then can you react correctly, even to point of mirroring. If they smile, return it with a warm open smile.

Resist any urge to fold any parts of your body, even if the other person does this. Be the leader and show an openness that reflects your honesty. That way they may begin to mirror you and you can be confident you have helped them to relax.

Proxemics – Space

Focus on how far apart you position yourself from the person you are speaking with. Don't enter their personal space, but don't be too far away that they have to raise their voice to be heard.

You should be conscious of your movements as you talk. This will be hard work as it goes against the grain of subconsciously reflecting your own emotions. Push aside those emotions for a short while. Convince yourself that you like the person you are communicating with. Do this even if you don't, or if they are strangers. That way your body language will stay open and loose. You never know, it may lead to a lifelong friendship or an important working acquaintance.

Chapter 12 Nonverbal Socializing

Social Groups

If we're capable of changing how others perceive us, does that mean we can make friends easier? Humans are also social creatures, so it's good to build up a circle of trustworthy friends and acquaintances.

Anthropologist, Robin Dunbar, studied apes whilst they interacted in social group settings. He was able to determine how many individuals were close in the group, such as grooming buddies, by the size of their neocortex of the brain. Chimps, for instance, have a social circle of around 50, but only 2 or 3 grooming friends. Humans have a larger neocortex than apes and chimps. So, by extrapolating the research, he surmised that we can maintain an outer social group of up to 150 people. Though, like the chimps, that number falls for close friendships to around 12 people. Another difference is that humans use language to bond, unlike chimps who use grooming.

It shows that our means of communicating enables us to build up larger social networks. There's nothing worse than having a false group of friends. People who let us down when we need them. Improve your communications skills to better understand body language. Then, you can then choose your friends wisely.

Manipulation In The Nicest Possible Way

Reading nonverbal movements that reveal a person's inner thoughts, is a powerful tool. In a sense, you can manipulate how other people perceive you, via your body language.

If we like a person we've met, not necessarily in a romantic way, we try harder to impress them. To make the correct judgments we need to understand more about their personality. By paying close attention to nonverbal reactions, it gives us the advantage to make the right choices.

This is a time when eye contact is important. If the other person averts their gaze from yours, then they're either not interested or they're a little shy. If you continue to use your improved communication skills, you can delve a little deeper and work out which reason it is

Use open body language to show that you have nothing to hide. Don't make rash or unexpected moves. It's far better to take your time with movements. No fidgeting or nervous twitches. Be transparent so other people get the impression that you're confident and in control. Don't over gesticulate when you speak. Keep your arms low and your movements slow. A calm controlled approach will help you come across as someone in control.

Continue to use that warm smile on and off so you appear friendly. If you feel the smile, you'll make yourself feel better too and this will come across as warm and inviting.

It's not all about the body language either. Monitor your own words, for example, when offering to buy the other person a drink, don't make it sound as if you're doing them a favor. Instead, make it sound like a friendly gesture, such as: "I'm about to order a drink, would you like one?"

With this approach, you are showing your willingness to "share." You are asking if they'd like to join you. If your body language is open as well, then you will be setting a relaxed scene as best you can. If they agree, this is your cue to shift a little bit closer into their personal space. Tread carefully because too much too soon could send the encounter into a downward spiral.

If a conversation ensues, make sure you listen to their words and respond to them with your body. Nodding your head in the right places is a good start. You have the advantage because you know that they will be watching your movements subconsciously. Lean closer towards them if you can. This is another gesture that you are taking an interest in what they have to say.

Another tactic is to mirror their movements but don't be too obvious. If they tilt their head, tilt yours a little too. Don't overdo it though, this is a fine line you are learning to walk.

The importance of mirroring can be seen in a study from 2008 (19). Using students in a negotiating situation, those who mirrored were successful in the test 67% of the time. Those who were not mirroring were only successful 12.5% of the time.

Once you feel the connection between, you can easily identify their mirroring of your actions. Try a yawn as this always works. Now you have a topic of humor to discuss, "erm...I think we both missed out on sleep last night, what's your story?" As they respond, lean in closer to listen to their words.

If they close up in their posture, such as crossing their arms or turning the top half of their body away, don't mirror. Such negative movements won't look good. You need to get the other person to relax. Show them your vulnerable regions, such as tilting your head back a little to expose your throat. Open up your hands and show your palms. By exposing yourself this way you are opening up to them.

By being observant and mirroring their behavior, you are putting yourself in sync with the other person. This will help to build up a rapport so you can identify with each other. If you can get in sync, you can pace the meeting on equal grounds. Whilst you're both evaluating each other, it is you who can lead the way. That's because you've taken the time to have a better understanding of the nonverbal clues. If you want a relationship to work, then bring out the best in yourself and the best in the other person.

Chapter 13 Four Distances In Body Language

Body language usually shows the extent of your feelings for someone. For instance, your feelings for another person, whether you like him or her as a friend or as a romantic interest, will show through your body language. Another important factor is the physical distance you observe from the person you are interacting with, since each relationship and social setting have their own recommended distance. Therefore, the next time you are in a conversation, take note of the distance you are keeping from someone. Your body language sends a stronger message than even the words that you are saying. People are very keen to read more into nonverbal signals than what comes out of the mouth.

To avoid being misunderstood, it is a good idea to learn about some of the common distances observed in nonverbal communication. You can then use the information you learn to nail your point home by sending the right message.

Intimate Distance

With this distance, you are supposed to observe a difference of 6 to 18 inches with your partner. This distance is usually reserved only for people who are intimate and have a strong affection for each other. This distance is enough to allow for actual touching, meaning there is a bigger opportunity to be closer to each other. Couples usually observe this distance when they are in public.

If you are dealing with a person that is not connected to you intimately, make sure to keep the proper distance because invading someone's personal space can be a disturbing gesture and can make them feel uncomfortable. Intimate distance is preserved for people who have close relationships, such as lovers, close family members, or even well-adored pets. In these cases, keeping a smaller distance helps to strengthen existing bonds.

Personal Distance

A distance of 1.5 to 4 feet is personal distance that is common between close friends and colleagues. You will always find people in deep conversation keeping this distance, especially as people are more able to observe their colleague or friend's body language. Expressions like movement of the eyes and lips send a very strong nonverbal message that shows the direction the conversation is going. It is very critical that the appropriate distance, based on the social setting, is strictly maintained.

If you want to shake hands, the personal distance is also appropriate, as it allows you enough space for this action, as well as any other physical gestures that you deem important in a casual social setting. This is due to the distance being able to cover the arm length, which is convenient when you are holding discussions as a group. You will not have any limitations to your movements, regardless of the number of people around you. There is enough space for your use and comfort is assured. Whenever you have associates and friends close to you for some discussions, ensure that you maintain a personal distance. When the appropriate personal distance is kept, people are more comfortable and at ease.

Social Distance

This distance requires two people to be 4 to 12 feet away from each other. Since this distance is more for social meetings, there is no need to keep a further distance away, such as the one you would keep for formal settings. In these settings, remember to also respect the positioning of the other people around you. Your body language and where you choose to position yourself in a room has a significant effect on how you are perceived by others. It is important to send across a humble, non-dominating, appearance so other people in the meeting can feel like they are being respected and heard. In social meetings, every person should be given an equal opportunity to participate.

Social distance is designed in such a way that maintaining eye contact among the people present is easy. Speeches delivered at social meetings should also be loud enough so that everyone can hear. Having the right amount of eye contact and voice volume can help to make communication a success. Without these essential elements, the effectiveness and productivity of social meetings will be lowered.

An additional note is that some social meetings can also be formal as well. Thus, there are exceptions to the distance of 4 to 12 feet. Knowing which distance is appropriate in which situation is crucial.

Public Distance

This distance measures 12 to 25 feet and comes into play in public meetings where one person is addressing a multitude. It is necessary to make sure the information being passed across can be received by all people without any exceptions. Additionally, at a public podium where the crowd may be more charged, this distance offers safety by shielding the speaker from possible attack. It is always good to keep a safe distance from people who might attack any time. However, considering the farther distance, public speakers standing 12 to 25 feet away from their audience are forced to mostly use exaggerated nonverbal gestures to effectively communicate their message to their audience. The speaker's message is most effective when his or her body language combines well with their spoken word.

At this distance, it will also be very difficult for the people to see the speaker's facial expressions. Thus, it becomes even more crucial for the speaker to effectively use gestures to add spark to his or her message. People who are experienced in public speaking and know how to read body languages will be very swift in making quick adjustments to suit their crowd or audience. For instance, experienced speakers will use larger hand or head gestures to substitute for their audience not being able to see their facial expressions at a far distance. Another example of someone who would keep a public distance is a teacher, who keeps a good space from students while teaching.

Now that you have learned about the different distances, you must choose the appropriate distance for the appropriate situation. Don't choose an intimate distance when you are speaking at a public gathering or vice versa. Understanding these nonverbal communication gestures will benefit you in many ways, whether it is personally or through your relationship with others. Understanding body language can help you better understand how other people are feeling in a situation. Being able to communicate good body language will also help you more effectively develop relationships, so others will take the time to know you and form a relationship with you.

Chapter 14 Interpreting And Responding To The Message

You've already learned how to analyze nonverbal language, but the key to excellent communications is knowing how to interpret and respond to the messages others send so that you can connect with them on a much more effective level. Wouldn't it be wonderful not to wonder what a person is thinking? Instead of questioning whether people are agreeable or accepting of your suggestions or opinions, you can use all the strategies you have learned in this book to look beyond the spoken word and read the hidden feelings people might be entertaining.

Some personality types are naturally more suited to one another, while others trigger feelings of annoyance and impatience, depending upon their key traits and character preferences. By examining each personality type a bit further, you'll gain some insight into why you instantly hit it off with some people and others just rub you the wrong way.

Leaders with Other Leaders

Partnering two Leader Personality Types is like putting two alpha dogs together in the same arena. Each one fights to lead, with nobody left to follow through and complete the task. With such competitive natures, Leaders struggle with one another to manipulate and control their environment. They are both sure their strategies and methodologies are the best, and compromise is not one of their strengths. For these reasons, placing two Leaders on a project can create unnecessary power plays, unless one's secondary personality type is a Fraternizer or Identifier.

When the relationship is personal, a coupling of two Leaders can be all work and no fun. If each is career-minded individuals, your lives will most likely not revolve around each other, but be centered on work-related events and projects. It is common when two career professionals hook up, for a while they will be quite intrigued by one another's focus and business acumen. However, as the relationship matures, the Leaders will tend to be more attentive to work-related issues, and their personal relationships suffer. If you are a Leader involved with another Leader Personality Type, you'll need to challenge one another on a personal level to keep the fires burning. Compete in a mutually enjoyed sport, or find a thrill-seeking, competitive hobby that interest both of you. It's necessary to be involved in one another's home life as well as your business endeavors.

Leaders with Perceivers

Leaders usually work well with Perceiver Personality Types because they are organizers and analytical thinkers, and their quiet, unemotional demeanor typically satisfies the Leader's goal-driven manner. The Perceiver doesn't challenge the Leader for "top dog" position because he or she doesn't enjoy being the center of attention. The downside to partnering a

Leader with a Perceiver is that the professional or personal relationship can be cold and rather unexciting unless there are some Fraternizer traits in one or the other's personality.

Leaders with Fraternizers or Identifiers

If the Fraternizers or Identifiers have some secondary Perceiver or Leader traits, they will do well when relating to people who are almost all Leader types. However, if the Fraternizer or Identifier is strong in their personality traits, their empathetic and emotional behaviors will often grate on the Leader's last nerve. What Fraternizers and Identifiers need to do when communicating with a Leader or Perceiver Types is to learn to curb their feelings and reign in their emotions when interacting with these strong personalities.

The two personality types that are usually not good to put together are Leader to Leader and Fraternizer to Fraternizer, and here's why. As we said before, two Leaders will fight for the controlling position. Examining the Fraternizers, they too are competitive, and they will experience a struggle unique to their type. Fraternizers will almost always try to one-up each other, challenging one another to a more dangerous sport or a project that requires greater and greater risks. Or, Fraternizers will turn everything into such fun that there will be no work accomplished. So, let's examine how to respond best to each personality type.

Communicating with an Identifier

Avoid getting too emotional when talking with an Identifier Personality Type. Since they are rather indecisive, you'll need to continually pull them back to the task at hand and discuss the decision to make and its' probably outcome. Identifiers enjoy talking about feelings, and they will be sensitive to yours. While this is good in a personal relationship, in the office it can be distracting.

If the Identifier is your direct report, their open-door policy will enable others to frequently interrupt your time with them, creating difficulties when trying to get them to stay on task. So, be patient; your frustration will not change their policies; it will only serve to make you look grumpy and cynical. After their interruptions, they'll be tempted to discuss the other person's problems with you, which will take you further down the rabbit hole. So, count on your meetings with Identifiers taking longer and achieving less.

There is almost always delays in projects as well. The Identifier will want you to check with other team members to see how they feel about any new ideas or changes, no matter how seemingly insignificant. Or, they will insist on discussing this issue in another meeting with more managers and team members. If you aren't careful, beginning a project can take a month of meetings.

In your personal relationships, Identifiers can be a bit moody and overly sensitive. If you are a Leader personality involved with a significant other who is an Identifier, you need to get comfortable with a relationship that is emotionally demanding. Also, your need to stay focused and move forward may make them feel as though they are not being heard or valued. As a Leader, you will need to slow down and allow the Identifier to fulfill his or her need to nurture and comfort. You won't be allowed to hide away when you're sick, and too many evenings spent working at the office is going to create some emotional outbursts.

Communicating with a Perceiver

Being in a personal relationship with a Perceiver Personality Type can be a guessing game. They don't like to share their feelings, and they can be a bit stand-offish, so if you are an Identifier that needs more reassurance, just know that you're not going to get it from the Perceiver. They might have deep feelings for you, but sharing those feelings is a challenge for them.

On the other hand, if you show too many emotions in the relationship, they'll be confused and draw further back into their comfortable, quiet shell of self-protection. Perceivers can also be rather stubborn and set in their ways, so getting them to change is like pulling teeth. If you do expect change, make sure you give them plenty of time to think things through and avoid popping any surprises on them, no matter how pleasant you think it will be for them to experience the change.

For example, Laurie decided it would be a great birthday present to replace her husband, Al's football chair. It was embarrassingly worn, and the springs were giving way, so she felt he would be much more comfortable watching his favorite programs in a nice, cushy, new recliner. As a surprise, Laurie had the new chair delivered while Al was at work, and they took the tattered one away. She didn't quite get the reaction she was hoping for when Al returned from work. Although he has never complained much about his old chair, Al has merely changed his favorite seating area to a corner of the couch.

Al might have liked the idea of having a new chair had Laurie not surprised him with the idea and had his old one hauled away before he was ready for the change. He needed time to adjust to the idea that another chair could be just as comfortable, and he could have gone to the store, sat in a gazillion chairs, then slowly made his mind up to purchase the first one in which he plopped. However, without having the opportunity to think it over, look at the chairs to decide which one best suited him, and then compare prices and warranties, Al was not thrilled with Laurie's birthday present.

Communicating with a Fraternizer

Fraternizer Personality Types can get along with almost anyone, but some personality types will eventually grow weary of their tired jokes and constant need for entertainment. Also, a Perceiver will not appreciate the spontaneous spending that many Fraternizers practice. A died-in-the-wool Fraternizer with few secondary personality traits that are more grounded is often too immature and impulsive for a Leader of Perceiver in their personal relationships.

In the workplace, Fraternizers are often perceived as party people and not taken seriously. No matter how intelligent, many Fraternizers are not promoted to their potential because they allow their fun-loving spirit too much free reign in the workplace. Fraternizers usually don't make good quarterly budget planners because they spend too freely and are too rash when it comes to decision-making. If you work with a Fraternizer, you will need to keep them focused and grounded to achieve success with projects in which you are both involved.

Examining Some Personal Scenarios

Think of a co-working with whom you are currently experiencing some challenges when communicating with him or her. Now review the following questions to determine the other person's personality type and what you can do to create a more positive working relationship.

- What is your subject's dominant personality type? How do you know this?

- What is your dominant personality type?

- What does this person do that annoys you? Analyze these behaviors to see if this is a trait of their personality type?

- What do you think you are doing that annoys him or her?

- Is this your imagination, or are you reading their non-verbal language?

- What was the last challenge you experienced with him or her?

- Based on his or her personality type, how could you have responded better to create a more positive outcome?

- Knowing what you know now, how will you communicate with this person in the future to create a better relationship?

Now, think of a personal relationship you would like to improve and ask yourself the same questions. When you determine the other's personality type, make sure you verify your beliefs by observing their behaviors, listening to their words, and analyzing the body language they are displaying around you. Ask yourself if you are too sensitive because of your personality type, or if you really are having serious communication issues with this person.

If you cannot answer the questions about people who challenge you, then keep reading.

The Method Behind The Madness

There're certain thing that you can't just change about yourself, however, & they're things that you can't really ignore, either. Sure, you can actually work around them... virtually everything in life can be worked with or around in some way, but they're still things that you need to be aware of. Not to mention the science behind anything is also simply fascinating, & it backs up the why behind it all.

First of all, let's take a moment to discuss hormones. The science of body language is also more evident in the outside appearance of any individual, but let me assure you, there's definitely more to it than meets the eye. There're certain hormones that're very much involved in how we react to things, & something as simple as the balance of hormones in one person's body can easily make them vastly different than another person.

There're two main hormones that're involved in this area of study. They're testosterone & cortisol.

The reason these're the two hormones of interest is because they're the two hormones that relate to leadership. A person that's an ideal leader has the perfect balance between these two hormones, & that isn't a 50/50 split, either.

To better understand what I mean, let's quickly take a look at each one separately, & put together what we find.

Testosterone is the dominance hormone

Almost all of us in life are familiar with Testosterone, at least to some extent. We all know that it's primarily a male hormone, but that women do have a level of it, too. We know that the more Testosterone a person actually has in their bloodstream, the more outspoken & aggressive they tend to be.

There's a reason for this, & that's because Testosterone is the dominance hormone. It's the hormone that's responsible for ruling over others, for elevating the confidence of the individual that has it, & for managing power.

It's a hormone that you can actually take supplements to get more of, but I recommend you hold off on that. The supplements are easily too much for your system, & you may end up with more problems than you want.

Cortisol is the stress hormone

The other hormone that's involved in this study is Cortisol. Now, Cortisol is the stress hormone. It's produced in both men & women equally, & it's produced when we feel stress.

You can also take other things to suppress this hormone in yourself, anti-depressants being one of those things, but again I just urge you to wait before you head for external interventions, as there're all kinds of ways you can manage these hormones without any outward help at all.

The reason I bring up these two hormones in particular is because they're the two hormones that show up in the testing of weak & powerful individuals.

There have been a number of tests done to try to determine the relationship between these two hormones in our bodies, & what we can do to balance them better.

The American Psychology Association ran a test on the two to basically determine how the mix of these hormones affects our social interactions. They say that the results varied, but in a study that was done by Princeton University, they actually found very consistent results.

Testosterone & Cortisol testing

In this test, 50 adults were taken into a room & had their baseline hormone levels taken. The results were recorded.

Then, they were directed to use power poses for 2 minutes

There're power poses that increase the feeling of power in our lives, & there're poses that decrease that feeling. The adults were all simply told how to hold themselves for the two minutes, & weren't shown which poses were linked to power or weakness.

They were also tested in seclusion, there wasn't anyone else in the room during these two minutes, & after the two minutes, they were all again tested for their hormone levels.

The results were astounding.

They found that all of the adults that were using the powerful power poses had an increase in Testosterone & a decrease in Cortisol. Also both levels had changed dramatically.

But here's where it also gets interesting. They found that in all of the adults that were in the weakened power poses, hormones had actually taken the opposite turn. Cortisol was actually higher in these people than it was before, & Testosterone had dropped.

This, of course, led the researchers and doctors to a whole new realm of questions.

If these adults responded to these poses after two minutes, is there a specific way that we can prepare ourselves for things that we need power for?

All they used was their own bodies & time... that's exactly what anyone has.

So, they quickly conducted another experiment.

The Job Interview Experiment

It took a while for the doctors to decide what test they ought to do next. They all wanted to have some sort of scenario that most anyone could relate to, & they finally decided that job interviewing was the way to go.

Most all of us have gone through that dreaded process, & most all of us dread having to do it again. With this in mind, they all decided that this was the best choice of scenario as it's the most relatable.

So again, they selected a number of adults to take part in the study, & they chose a single person to conduct the mock interviews. The person that was actually conducting the interviews was to remain expressionless the entire time. Studies also actually show that we as people can't stand to talk to someone with no expression. We'd rather be ridiculed, made fun of, yelled at, or even pretty much anything besides dealing with lack of expression.

So again this new set of adults was quickly instructed to go into these power poses for two minutes. They were to do this in the other room, alone, & wait for their turn in the interview. People out of sight watched & analyzed how the interview went from behind glass.

Again, the results were consistent & astounding. The people that engaged in the powerful power poses from the beginning were the ones that were all confident in the room. They were open, outspoken, relaxed, & clearly more at ease than the people that were in the weaker power poses.

Upon further examination, these doctors realized that when most of us are waiting for a job interview, we're in the weakest pose while waiting. This actually does nothing for our confidence level except to damage it, & if we want to see better results in the interview room. We've to break this cycle.

When you're waiting for a job interview, what do you do? We simply tend to sit with our arms crossed. We perhaps look down at our phones or our notes, we cross our legs. Those're all things we subconsciously do when we feel insecure... which, as we learned already, if we do things that essentially make us feel a certain way, it's only a matter of time before we start to really feel that way.

With that in mind, you can easily see how sitting this way before your job interview is going to negatively affect how it goes.

But, there's good news! If you want it to go better, you can see by these examples here proven facts that you can do things that'll increase your confidence.

Ok, I can see how this all works together, but you said earlier that powerful people have a good balance of Testosterone & Cortisol. What exactly is that balance then?

A lot of people think that the more Testosterone they have, the better off they'll be. They think they'll be powerful, confident, tough, & able to move anything & everything out of their way. The problem with hormone supplements, however, is that it only raises one hormone, but actually doesn't do anything to the others.

You see, if you're a person that's highly stressed out, & you think you want to be more confident, the worst thing you can do is add Testosterone into your life. You're then going to feel rough & tough, but also incredibly stressed out.

Your stress is going to go up even further as you feel this way, because you'll stress about why it isn't working. You'll be more defensive, you won't feel any of the positives out of this experience, which, in turn, won't actually give you that confidence you need.

Power is also how you react to stress

It's a mistake to think that power is all glory. You're going to have your fair share of stress in life, no matter who you're or what position you hold. In fact, it seems that the more powerful a person is in life, the more stressful situations arise.

The key to effective power is to just react to stress well. You can't ever eliminate it from your life, but you can learn how to respond to it in a healthy & non-invasive way. If you do this, you'll feel your Testosterone levels increase, but at the same time your Cortisol levels are going to decrease. The combination of this's the exact match you're hoping for.

When you balance these two levels in this way, you'll actually begin to feel powerful, & your confidence is going to rise.

Your increased confidence is then just going to cause you to hold yourself in a powerful way, telling the world you're a confident person, just through your body language.

Tying it all together

There's a lot of information here that's very important to understand, but to summarize it now, you can see that:

You can manage your hormone levels by just doing certain poses for a few minutes in a day. The better you're able to manage your hormone levels, the more confident you're going to feel.

The more confident you feel, the more your body is going to carry itself with confidence, which's going to balance out your hormone levels.

As you can see here, this's going to start in you a cycle, & that cycle is going to keep you in the powerful & confident mindset you're looking for.

So with this understanding in mind, let's move on to how you can effectively put this into practice, & start to build up that confidence in yourself.

Conclusion

Body language is incredibly important. Most of the feelings you give to other people will come about through your body language – 55% of them in fact. It is important to take great notice of your body language – if you fail to, there is a good chance you will accidentally make people dislike and distrust you.

For example, if you tell someone you're glad to see them while fidgeting and looking at the ground... they may not trust that you mean what you're saying.

Your body language will also cause other people's first (and lasting) impression of you. If their first impression of you is of an unconfident, uncomfortable, beta male – that impression is very unlikely to change.

The first steps to becoming the strong, confident man you want to be is to start taking up the body language that a strong, confident man would take. In time, that body language will become natural and your authentic body language.

Most importantly, the body language you take up will have a real, physical impact on you. By looking like a strong, confident alpha male – you will start to become a strong, confident alpha male.

So taking the time to fake it is worth it because after a while, you won't be faking it anymore!

Once you start putting this into action you will find that women will start to act a lot more interested in you. That is because finding an alpha male is like gold dust to women, there just aren't enough out there to go around. So as soon as they find you they will never want to let you go, it'll be like they are addicted to you!

Even when you are just "faking it" you will notice a difference, but when you become it. Well, that's when the good stuff starts.

Of course, as good as all of this sounds – it won't happen until you get started. Because, while this all this knowledge is great, it isn't worth anything if you don't actually do something with it! Remember, the sooner you start, the sooner you will become the alpha male you want to be.

All you need to do is get out there and get started today!

If this book has been useful to you and you like it, I suggest you also read these my books

"How to analyze people"

"Manipulation psychology"

"Persuasion Skills"

www.ingramcontent.com/pod-product-compliance
Lightning Source LLC
Chambersburg PA
CBHW070708250726
48662CB00001B/314